# SQUADRONS!

## No. 17

## The Curtiss
# Mohawk

Phil H. LISTEMANN

**ISBN: 979-10-96490-00-4**



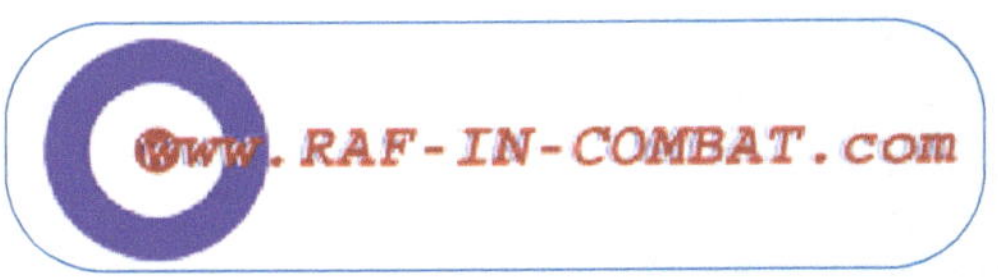


**Colour profiles: Gaetan Marie/Bravo Bravo Aviation**



*Contributors & Acknowledgments:*

*Stefaan Bouwer, Paul Sortehaug, Andrew Thomas*

## Glossary of Terms

Personel :

(aus)/RAF: Australian serving in the RAF
(bel)/RAF: Belgian serving in the RAF
(can)/RAF: Canadian serving in the RAF
(cz)/RAF: Czechoslovak serving in the RAF
(nfl)/RAF: Newfoundlander serving in the RAF
(nl)/RAF: Dutch serving in the RAF
(nz)/RAF: New Zealander serving in the RAF
(pol)/RAF: Pole serving in the RAF
(rho)/RAF: Rhodesian serving in the RAF
(sa)/RAF: South African serving in the RAF
(us)/RAF - RCAF : American serving in the RAF or RCAF

Ranks

G/C : Group Captain
W/C : Wing Commander
S/L : Squadron Leader
F/L : Flight Lieutenant
F/O : Flying Officer
P/O : Pilot Officer
W/O : Warrant Officer
F/Sgt : Flight Sergeant
Sgt : Sergeant
Cpl : Corporal
LAC : Leading Aircraftman

Other

ATA: Air Transport Auxiliary
CO : Commander
DFC : Distinguished Flying Cross
DFM : Distinguished Flying Medal
DSO : Distinguished Service Order
Eva. : Evaded
ORB : Operational Record Book
OTU : Operational Training Unit
PoW : Prisoner of War
PAF: Polish Air Force
RAF : Royal Air Force
RAAF : Royal Australian Air Force
RCAF : Royal Canadian Air Force
RNZAF : Royal New Zealand Air Force
SAAF : South African Air Force
s/d: Shot down
Sqn : Squadron
† : Killed

### Codenames - Offensive Operations - Fighter Command

***Circus:***
Bombers heavily escorted by fighters, the purpose being to bring enemy fighters into combat.

***Ramrod:***
Bombers escorted by fighters, the primary aim being to destroy a target.

***Ranger:***
Large formation freelance intrusion over enemy territory with aim of wearing down enemy figthers.

***Rhubard:***
Freelance fighter sortie against targets of opportunity.

***Rodeo:***
A fighter sweep without bombers.

***Sweep:***
An offensive flight by fighters designed to draw up and clear the enemy from the sky.

# The Curtiss Mohawk

The Curtiss Hawk 75 was the export version of the USAAC Curtiss P-36 that became, from 1936 onwards, the standard American single-seat fighter and represented a big step forward for the USAAC. The French were the first to express interest in this fighter when they sent a purchase commission to the USA in 1938. At that time, the French knew that another war with Germany was imminent and rearming the air force had become a necessity. However, the French manufacturers encountered huge problems in delivering the massive orders placed by the Government. Until the French aviation industry could deliver the aircraft ordered and new types under testing could be put in to service, the search for new aircraft went overseas. Consequently, many types were ordered from the Americans with the Curtiss H-75 being the first. An initial order for 100 Curtiss H-75A-1s in September 1938 was followed by another contract for 100 Curtiss H-75A-2s in March 1939. When war broke out, a third contract was signed in October 1939 for 530 Curtiss H-75A-3s but this was later amended to 400 in March 1940. The machines of this last batch were intended to be powered by an updated version of the R-1830 engine installed in the aircraft of the previous two batches. However, at that time, Pratt & Whitney was facing production problems with high demand for its R-1830 and, eventually, only 135 of Hawks would receive the R-1830. The French, therefore, decided upon an alternative, the Wright Cyclone, for the last 285 aircraft. They were delivered as H-75A-4s while, at the same time, a part of the last order was amended to include Curtiss H-81As (the export version of the P-40). So, in all, 620 Curtiss H-75s were ordered, of which all of the A-1s, A-2s and A-3s had been delivered when France collapsed in June 1940. As for the A-4, the first examples had reached French soil before the Armistice and some even took part in the last days of the Battle of France.

When the French ask for an armistice, all of the contracts were taken over by the British Purchase Commission and the denominations of Mohawk Mk. I, II, III and IV were chosen for the four variants ordered by the French (H-75A-1 to A-4). No Curtiss H-75A-1s or A-2s would ever reach the UK and the denomination was therefore never used. No A-3s reached England either but five H-75A-6s, the Norwegian export version of the H-75A-3, did. These were on their way to Norway when that country was invaded by Germany in June 1940. They would become the only examples of the Mohawk Mk. III to see RAF service. In the meantime, Curtiss continued to produce the Curtiss H-75A-4 for the British who had to organise their shipment to Britain, something easier said than done in the summer of 1940 due to the lack of available shipping assets. To simplify the production and to avoid unwanted delays, the H-75A-4s were built to the French standard and were shipped to the UK in sequence when ships did become available. Therefore, the first Curtiss H-75A-4s reached British soil at the end of July 1940. Upon arrival, a RAF serial number was allocated and the aircraft converted to RAF standard to become Mohawk IVs. One of the significant changes was to the throttle operation. Contrary to British and American practice, the French pulled the throttle back to increase power. Despite this and other changes, the Mohawk would remain a hybrid aircraft as, for example, the instruments and gauges were left as per the French standard and, therefore, reported their readings using metric measures (metres, kilometres etc). This explains why the serials are spread out over

Mohawk AR631, a former Norwegian H-75A-6, was used by the A&AEE between November 1940 and June 1941 to test flight the Mk. III variant. It became an instructional airframe in September 1941 and was struck off charge in October 1945.

Above, another Mk. III, AR634. Note that the H-75A-6 had only two wing guns, like the first H-75 models (see below, AR634 taken from the front), and not four like the last models. On the other hand, the bomb racks are partially installed. AR634 was briefly studied by Westlands between August and October 1940. It would continue to fly as a hack in various places until the end of July 1944 when it was stored before being scrapped the following November. Note the paint scheme.

various sequences. The last Curtiss H-75A-4 left the production line at the end of August 1940 but was only taken on by the RAF in March 1941 only. The French H-75s taken on charge received the serials **AR635 to AR694**, **AX880 to AX898**, **BB918 to BB937**, **BB974 to BB979**, **BJ434 to BJ453**, **BJ531 to BJ550**, **BK569 to BK588**, **BK876 to BK879**, **BL220 to BL223**, **BS730 to BS738**, **BS744 to BS747**, **BS784 to BS798** and **BT470 to BT472**. These corresponded to the French Air Force numbers of 65 to 78, 91, 95 and 98 to 285. The Norwegian H-75A-6s, which had been stored disassembled since their arrival, were uncrated with the first batch of A-4s and allocated the serials **AR630 to AR634**. In all, 204 Curtiss H-75A-4s were taken on charge by the RAF.

To complicate things, the RAF would also receive more Hawks from various sources later on. When the British occupied Persia in August 1941, they found ten Hawk H75-A-9 still in their crates. This version was close to the French A-4 and had been ordered the previous year by the Persians. Nine of them were seized by the RAF and were logically included in the RAF inventory as Mohawk IVs with serials **LA157 to LA165**. Unlike their French counterparts, however, they were never fully converted to RAF standard but were considered good enough to serve as advanced trainers in India. Another unexpected batch was also partially taken on charge.

It had been intended that the Curtiss H-75A-5 (Chinese export version of the A-4) would be assembled in China at Lowing, close to the Burmese border. Due to the Japanese invasion of Burma, supplies could not be delivered to the factory and it was eventually agreed with the Chinese that the supplies intended for Lowing, and those salvaged from there after Japanese bombing raids, would be transferred to Hindustan Aircraft Ltd in India. An order was placed for 48 aircraft and serials **DR761 to DR808** were reserved for this batch. Only five were actually built as Mohawk IVs with the rest cancelled when Hindustan Aircraft Ltd was required to transfer its energies to the maintenance of USAAF and RAF aircraft serving in India. It is suspected that the RAF used these aircraft as advanced trainers in OTUs because they were slightly different from the Mohawk IVs based on the French aircraft. The RAF also received two more Mohawks, **AX799**, which was the pattern aircraft built by Curtiss as part of the agreement for the Chinese A-5 production, and **HK823**, a former French Curtiss H-75A-3 whose pilot had fled from French Africa in February 1941. The latter would never use the denomination Mohawk III as it was never converted to RAF standard. The final total of Curtiss H-75s taken on charge by the RAF was 225.

### General RAF usage:

The Curtiss Mohawks that arrived in the UK were initially stored after their conversion to basic RAF standard (further modifications were made later) and no decision was made on their use for some time as the RAF had enough Hurricanes and Spitfires on hand throughout 1940 and 1941. The first trials also showed that the overall performance of the Mohawk was inferior to the two main RAF fighter types and it was under-armed with six light machine guns instead of the eight installed in the Hurricane or the Spitfire. It was decided that the aircraft would not be used operationally in the UK except in the case of an emergency. For the five Mk. IIIs, no extensive usage was possible because of the small number on hand. The relatively large numbers of Mk. IVs, however, did lend themselves to useful employment. In the beginning of 1941, it was decided to use the Mohawk overseas with a breakdown as follows: ninety to the Middle East, ninety to the SAAF (which was looking for modern fighter types in numbers), and 24 to a fighter squadron at Aden. Plans were later altered, with the SAAF actually receiving seventy of the promised ninety and the rest serving in Egypt with none sent to Aden. However, many of the aircraft sent to the Middle East actually continued their journey to India where they were joined by the ex-Persian and Indian Mohawks. In all, about ninety reached India and two fighter squadrons would eventually become operational on the type in 1942. With the Persian and Chinese models, about 100 Mohawks served in India. The same year, 1941, Great Britain provided fifteen (of sixteen initially planned) to Portugal and these were delivered between August and October 1941 while a

Mohawk IV AR644 was one of the Mohawks of this type test flown by the RAF. A year after the end of the trials in December 1940, it was sent to India only to be lost in April 1942. Note the change in the design of the cowling compared to the Mk. III.

Mohawk Mark IV, BK585, running up its engine prior to giving a flying demonstration at the Aeroplane and Armament Experimental Establishment, Boscombe Down, Wiltshire. BK585 joined No. 5 Squadron in the Far East later in 1941. BK585 is camouflaged as applied between November 1940 and April 1941 with the port wing painted in black Night.

couple continued to fly in the UK with second-line units. In the same time six Mohawks which have been found damaged on arrival and needed repairs were struck off charge and were reduced to components (AR639, AR643, AR647, AR673, AR687 and BK576) in November and December 1941. Needless to say that the Mohawks were totally obsolete when they were introduced to operations in 1942 against the Japanese. It was a good stop-gap measure, however, before Hurricanes began to arrive in significant numbers. In 1942, RAF fighter squadrons were fighting over Malta, over the Continent, and reinforcements were needed in Australia and in the Far East, stretching the RAF's capacities to its limits. The Mohawk, therefore, was welcomed. It would be used against the Japanese until the end of 1943 in the fighter and fighter-bomber role and, despite its total obsolescence, gave a surprisingly good account (seventeen kills) over about 2,000 sorties flown against at least 35 aircraft lost to all causes by the two operational units, Nos 5 & 155 Sqns even if doubt still exist regarding the real cause of about ten premature striking off.

Mohawk AR645 missed its chance somewhere. Stored for a long time after its arrival in UK, it was earmarked for the Far East in May 1942 but the move was cancelled. Instead, it joined the CRD (Controller of Research & Development) until the end of February 1943. It was the last Mk. IV still flying in the UK by that time. It flew unarmed and it is clear that the MGs were disposed of. AR645 was finally shipped to the Far East and arrived in November 1943 when the type was close to being withdrawn. It was probably, therefore, never issued to any unit. As with the other Mohawks still in RAF hands in the Far East, it was stricken from the inventory on 1 March 1944. This photo is officially dated September 1942.

# December 1941
# July 1943

**Victories - confirmed or probable claims: 11.0**

**First operational sortie:**
**16.06.42**
**Last operational sortie:**
**24.05.43**

**Number of sorties:** *ca.***1225**

**Total aircraft written-off: 18**

Aircraft lost on operations: 8
Aircraft lost in accidents: 10

## Squadron code letters:
# OQ

(until end 1942, then nil)

### Commanding Officers

| | | | | |
|---|---|---|---|---|
| S/L James R. Maling | RAF No. 37049 | (NZ)/RAF | ... | 02.03.42 |
| S/L John H. Giles | RAF No. 37851 | RAF | 02.03.42 | 17.06.42 |
| S/L William Pitt-Brown | RAF No. 33348 | RAF | 17.06.42 | 11.11.42 |
| S/L Peter McC. Bond | RAF No. 40073 | RAF | 11.11.42 | 08.03.43 |
| S/L Guy J.C. Hogan | RAF No. 40912 | RAF | 08.03.43 | ... |

## Squadron Usage

Number 5 Squadron was the first RAF fighter squadron to receive the Mohawk. Up until that time, the squadron had been based in India but was serving as an Army Co-operation unit flying Hawker Audaxes. As it soon became clear to the RAF that more fighter squadrons were to be based in India for air defence duties, it was decided to convert 5 Squadron to a fighter role early in 1941. However, the pilots had to wait until the end of November to attend a short conversion course at Bangalore. At that time, the squadron could count on about fifteen pilots under the command of S/L James R. Maling, a New Zealander serving in the RAF. Between 11 and 15 December, the squadron moved to Dum Dum to take over the defence of Calcutta. There, pending the delivery of the Mohawk, all of the Audaxes were converted into single-seat fighters. The first Mohawk was actually delivered on 29 December (flown by Sgt Campbell). As more Mohawks arrived at the squadron in January, training increased and so did the accidents. On 17 January, Sgt Bates made a forced-landing in AR677 due to shortage of petrol. The aircraft was repaired. The next day, F/L E.C. Fyson landed at Dum Dum with the undercarriage partially lowered, causing enough damage to the aircraft, BJ438, that it would be struck off charge in August 1942. In April and March, more Mohawks and pilots arrived at the squadron, allowing the unit to hand over some of its Audaxes to No. 146 Squadron. On 2 March, the squadron had a change of command with S/L John H. Giles replacing S/L Maling (he would later become OC No. 619 Squadron on Lancaster and ended the war as a PoW). One month later, while practicing circuits in AR678, Sgt Charles T. Kronk (RNZAF on detachement from No. 67 Sqn) undershot the runway at Dum Dum and crashed due to a lack of landing speed and a late application of power. The Mohawks were repairable and sent to No. 301 MU, but it seems no repairs were undertaken and the aircraft were re-categorised 'E' in August.On 25 April, the squadron lost a Mohawk when W/C Stephen, while conducting a familiarisation flight, was the victim of an oil system failure after a fast

Bill Pitt-Brown, or 'PB', was a regular RAF officer flying Vickers Valentia bomber-transport aircraft in India when war broke out. He then served as an instructor training Indian Air Force pilots. He joined 5 Sqn after the Japanese invasion. After his tour ended in April 1943 (as 169 Wing wing leader), he was awarded the DFC in May. He was sent to England afterwards and eventually reverted to squadron leader and became OC 174 Sqn, flying Typhoons, in 2 TAF. He was then posted as wing leader of No. 121 Wing in August 1944 and stayed in that role until October 1944. He served in the RAF after the war. *(Andrew Thomas)*

Mohawk BJ546 was one of the first Mohawks to be issued to 5 Sqn, but its career would be short as it was lost on a tactical reconnaissance on 24 May 1942. BJ546 is wearing the 'OQ' codes that would be discontinued at the end of the year. *(CV Bargh via P. Sortehaug)*

climb to 10,000 feet and subsequent dive at about 300 mph. The oil entered the cockpit and Stephen had no choice but to abandon the Mohawk at 4,000 feet. The oil system of the Mohawk was to cause much trouble during the type's service in the RAF.

On 5 May, a major change occurred when aircraft, pilots and about fifty ground personnel proceeded to Dinjan, in north-eastern India not far from the Burmese border, where they joined the remainder of No. 146 Squadron, while the remaining ground echelon left at Dum Dum was re-named 146 Squadron. The ORB is incomplete for May until mid-June, and many pages are missing, so it is difficult to know what exactly happened. However, it was far from a quiet month with no less than four Mohawks were lost and three pilots posted missing. The first loss occurred on 17 May when, during a non-operational flight, possibly a test flight, the engine cut in flight and oiled up the windshield. The pilot, P/O Jonathan Rashleigh, made a crash-landing and escaped injury. The aircraft, BS786, however was not so fortunate and was declared unrepairable on 10 August and converted to components. The next day, the squadron lost another Mohawk, believed to be during a tactical reconnaissance, when F/S Robert D. Cameron, a son of British parents living in Kenya, lost control in cloud and dived into the ground. Neither the aircraft nor the pilot was ever found and this loss was attributable to the lack of sufficient blind flying instruments. Two more Mohawks were also posted missing on 24 May during a tactical reconnaissance. Flight Sergeant Christopher G. Campbell and Sgt Alan T. Wood were both posted missing, presumed dead. They probably collided in cloud during the flight. On 17 June, S/L William Pitt-Brown became the CO replacing Giles who was later posted to the UK and would become OC 90 Squadron on Stirling in 1943. Pitt-Brown was a regular RAF officer who had, so far, only served in India. In June, few details were provided regarding operations after the 16th. It is all rather sketchy. What is known is that six Mohawks led by the CO provided an escort to three No. 113 Squadron Blenheims on 18 June to attack the aerodrome of Myitkyina. No air opposition was encountered. The next day, the squadron lost two more Mohawks in a collision during a training flight. Flight Sergeant Errol W.J. Blake, from the Irish Republic, perished in the crash, but P/O T. J. Trimble bailed out to safety. Bad weather for the rest of the month prevented flying and when it improved it was only enough to allow local flights. Likewise for the first days of July and it was not until the 6th that an armed reconnaissance over Myitkyina aerodrome was flown. No activity was recorded, but targets of opportunity were strafed. The next day, four Mohawks took off at 12.45 to attack Japanese positions and dropped forty 20-lb bombs. As no reliable documents are available for the previous weeks, it seems that this was the first time the Mohawk was used as a fighter-bomber. From now on, the Mohawk would be mainly used as a fighter-bomber against Japanese positions and almost all of the sorties completed in July were

Mohawk BB975 was also an early allotment to 5 Sqn, but it would end its career in November 1943 while serving with 155 Sqn. Among the first Mohawks to have been issued with BB975/OQ-X were : AR677/OQ-D, AR678, BB976, BJ542, BJ438, BJ544, BJ546/OQ-O, BK578.

Mohawk BJ441 was initially earmarked for the SAAF in December 1941 and shipped in January 1942, but it seems it was diverted to India before reaching its initial destination. BJ441 is seen here with 5 Sqn codes but they are now painted in black. It was to be SOC in February 1944. *(Andrew Thomas)*

fighter-bomber ops. These were low scale operations with each comprising between one and four aircraft. During the month, the squadron received some fresh pilots in the form of three New Zealanders and one Canadian.

In August, with the weather improving, the number of sorties increased significantly with close to 100 achieved mainly in the fighter-bomber role, and little was seen of the Japanese Army Air Force. However on 20 August, five Mohawk were sent out for an offensive reconnaissance. Returning from the mission a single-engined aircraft was sighted flying along a river in the opposite direction. Sergeant Stuart Barnett made a 180-degree descending turn to the right and then closing the distance. Garnett opened fire at 100 yards stoping when it was at 30 yards. The Japanese aircraft, a Ki-36 (but identified as a Ki-27) was seen to go into a medium dive with smoke and flames coming from the cockpit. The pilot baled out at 1,000 feet and landed on the top of a tree. It was the first air victory for an RAF Mohawk. During the month, the 5 also flew other kind of missions as escorts from time to time, like on 25 August when twelve Mohawks escorted three Blenheims detailed to attack Myitkyina aerodrome. The next day, eight bombed up Mohawks took off for

F/Sgt 'Rod' Lawrence, one of the Canadians of 5 Sqn at the end of 1942, used to fly BB925 (coded 'R') and decorated it with a large red maple leaf with the head of a timber wolf superimposed. He also named BB925 'Rod and Lois' after his wife. Lawrence was to be the first squadron pilot to make a claim while flying the Mohawk, in this aircraft, on 7 October. *(Andrew Thomas)*

Myitkyina once again. Bombs were dropped and ground targets strafed and the formation returned without having sustained any damage. However, while landing at Dinjan, the undercarriage of AX896 collapsed. The pilot, Sgt J.R. Bates, was unharmed. First categorised 'E', unrepairable, it was later changed to 'B' and, it seems, the aircraft was repaired. That month, new pilots arrived at the squadron and on 31 August, the unit could now count on 26 pilots. In all, they logged 440 hours of flight, all but a few on Mohawks, and 284 of those were flown on operations. In September, due to bad weather, activity dropped off, with half the number of sorties flown compared to the previous month. During the last week of the month the Mohawks were called upon a couple of times to intercept enemy aircraft flying over the aerodrome, but all attempts to engage failed. The last day of September was the biggest when twelve Mohawks took-off to attack enemy aircraft that had been spotted at the Akyab satellite aerodrome. The target was bombed and strafed and the pilots noticed that some dummy aircraft had been seemingly constructed from British wrecks as roundels could be still seen. During the raid, one Mohawk (AX895), flown by Sgt William G. Thomas, hit trees while flying low and he was seen to crash on the airfield. He was posted missing even though there was no doubt about his real fate. For the month, the air activity was totalled 390 hours of which eighty were flown on operations.

On 1 October, a new wing was formed with the two Mohawk squadrons, Nos. 5 and 155. This was part of a major restructure for the RAF in the Far East with the formation of other wings. Squadron Leader Bill Pitt-Brown was selected as wing leader and he left the squadron on the 14th for his new position. He was replaced by S/L Peter McC Bond who officially took over on 11 November. At the same time, the squadron was relocated south at Agartala, near Dacca. Otherwise, air activity remained constant in October. On the 3rd, while practicing a cross-country, Sgt P. Cutfield (RNZAF) became lost. He soon ran out of fuel and was obliged to make an emergency landing which ended well for him, but not for the Mohawk as it was wrecked. On the 7th, the Mokawks returned to Akyab with ten aircraft to provide escort to Blenheims of Nos. 60 and 113 Squadrons. As the fighters were refuelling at Feni, a Japanese reconnaissance aircraft passed overhead indicating a possible raid. The pilots rushed to take-off and headed to the target area. Once there, the Mohawks saw Japanese aircraft flying above and thought they had taken off to avoid being destroyed on the ground. Actually, the British arrived at the time a cargo vessel carrying supplies was approaching and the Japanese aircraft (Ki-48 'Lilys') were airborne on patrol. In seeing the British fighters, the enemy dispersed and two headed out to sea. Flight Sergeant 'Rod' Lawrence RCAF attacked one of them and, on his third pass, was able to set fire to the left engine. The 'Lily' dived to the right and crashed into the sea. The same day, led by F/L Lee, W/O E. Worts and Sgt Gore went for patrol from which Worts did not come back. The next day, he was able to send words explaining that he was obliged to make a forced landing near Begunkudar and was injured. Otherwise, the rest of the month was rather uneventful and, in all, 285 hours were carried out in October, 107 of them on operations. Between 1 and 6 November, no flying activity was recorded. On the 6th and 7th, the squadron was tasked with maintaining cover for a ship departing Chittagong harbour, but no incidents occurred. The next action took place three days later after all flying activity was prevented by heavy storms once more. The squadron was called to provide escort nine Blenheims from Nos. 60 and 113 Squadrons to attack Akyab docks from 5,000 feet. Eight Mohawks were provided, four acting as close escort flying at 4,500 feet while the other four flew high cover at 14,000 feet. The way in was uneventful, as was the attack as such, but soon after dropping their bombs, the Blenheims were attacked by about seven or eight Japanese fighters. The close cover reacted quickly to protect the bombers. Sergeant Francis Gore carried out a quarter attack from

Squadron codes were discontinued by the end of 1942 as only two units were flying the Mohawk. Number 5 Squadron chose to put the individual letter to the rear of the roundel while 155 did the opposite. The individual letter here is painted in black. AR690 was struck off charge on 1 March 1944. It was usually flown by F/Sgt Derek Wicks (here leaning into the cockpit). The other pilot is P/O Harold Seifert, a RCAF pilot who would be killed in November 1943. Note 'The Saint' painted on the nose. *(Andrew Thomas)*

The two sides of BB977, coded 'Black D', in January 1943. It was lost soon after in a fatal crash while on a test flight. Note the yellow wing tips.

astern on a Ki-43 and fired at a range of 200 yards. He saw strikes entering the aircraft, its windscreen shattered and thick white smoke came from the exhaust. The aircraft was seen to stall and dive at a very steep angle to the sea. Gore claimed it as a probable. Pilot Officer Richard Tovey made several attacks too, damaging one, then got on the tail of one and, after a long burst, streams of white vapour were seen. He was distracted by a resounding when at that point, another aircraft collided with the tail of his aircraft and he went into a spin. He was only able to recover at the last moment before safely returning to base. The CO had spotted the loose formation of Ki-43s at 9,000 feet when the engagement began. His radio failed so he could not call in the other Mohawks. He therefore attacked alone and reported one enemy aircraft crashed into the sea. At the same time, F/L David Cunliffe saw a Blenheim under attack and went to its aid. In the ensuing combat, he claimed two Japanese fighters as damaged. Now it was the high cover's turn to be engage. While F/L McEwan and Sgt Boyles maintained a watchful eye from above, F/L D.F. Bullen and P/O W.J. Lee dived from 14,000 feet and entered the fight. Bullen and Lee both claimed one Ki-43 as damaged but Bullen's aileron and rudder were hit and he decided to return to Agartala with a much less controllable aircraft. Soon after, the combat ended with a good tally for the squadron of two enemy aircraft destroyed, one probable and five damaged. For the rest of the month, the unit was called at various times to provide escort to single aircraft or to scramble to intercept enemy aircraft (but without any success). On 24 November, one Mohawk was wrecked when Sgt T.G. Smith made a belly landing returning from a practice flight with flaps and undercarriage jammed. Smith was unlucky as he made his landing alongside the runway while a Blenheim was also landing amid a cloud of dust. With poor visibility, Smith did his best but the outcome was anything but good. The aircraft was a total write-off and Smith suffered facial injuries, a fractured jaw and lost one eye. His career as a pilot was over. The next day, it was the turn of P/O Beyts to have an accident (in BK585) but the consequences weren't as bad for both aircraft and pilot as returned to service quickly. When November ended, the figures testified that despite the bad weather of the first few days, the squadron had been able to fly 585 hours that month with an impressive 490 of them on operations. It was easily the best month so far. December would be even better with 800 hours flown, including 725 on operations, but much of it required flying boring patrols with just some escorts of Blenheims or Hurricanes and some rare offensive operations mounted from Imphal, like on Christmas Day, to spice things up a little.

1943 began on the 2nd with an escort of five Blenheims in conjunction with 155 Squadron. It was an attack on Akyab aerodrome again. The following week saw little activity and the squadron had to wait until the 11th to participate in an operation, where six aircraft were needed, joining six Blenheims and six Hurricanes to bomb Pyintha. The Mohawks then continued to Kyaikthin where thirty-one 40-lb bombs were dropped on the railways and town area. Four days later, F/O Bellinger, F/Sgt Baines and Sgt Worts were airborne from Imphal for another Rhubarb mission. From 1,500 feet, they dropped seven 40-lb bombs on railways and a factory at Hopin, succeeding in setting one building on fire. Targets of opportunity were then strafed. This mission had a cost, however, as F/O Peter Bellinger's BK572 was hit by ground fire and he force-landed north of Mohnyin, east of Bilunyo. He was seen to get out of his aircraft before it burst into flames. He was eventually captured. The Mohawks of the squadron were out on the 19th escorting 113 Squadron Blenheims to Akyab once more. They observed eight to ten Japanese aircraft that had been sent up to intercept. One section attacked the Japanese while the six other Mohawks continued with the Blenheims before joining in the dogfight which had developed with the now identified Ki-43s. The engagement lasted twenty to thirty minutes during which F/L David Cunliffe, who had recently been awarded the DFC for his actions with the squadron the previous summer, claimed one Ki-43 as destroyed. This later became a probable. Indeed, although he saw his burst hitting the cockpit area of his opponent, and saw the aircraft diving vertically, smoking, he was unable to give the location of the impact. Flying Officer 'Smokey' Boyes (from Brazil of British parentage) claimed one Ki-43 damaged and then turned his guns on another that was attacking a Mohawk. Just as he was about to break away, the 'Oscar' dived abruptly and its tail swung up and struck his right wing. On return to base, a piece about four feet long was removed from the wingtip and a piece of the tail unit of the Ki-43 was left embedded in the broken end. The Mohawk would be struck off charge two days later after investigation. As F/L Cunliffe saw the Japanese aircraft crashing, it was claimed as destroyed and, for his part, F/O Mendizabel claimed two more as damaged. Three days later, the squadron was part of an operation to attack Prome airfield in conjunction with Hurricanes. The Mohawks dive-bombed with 20-lb bombs. Having done so, the pilots then spotted a lone bomber

Mohawk BS796/T was the personal mount of the new CO, S/L Bond. This aircraft would later serve with 155 Sqn. Note the squadron leader pennant and the personal artwork painted on the nose. *(Andrew Thomas)*

Mohawk BK573/G at dispersal. The bomb racks are clearly visible here. BK573 was later passed to 155 Sqn. Note the personal artwork on the nose, a white winged horse. This Mohawk arrived at the squadron on 21 November 1942 with AR690 (see previous page), AR662, BB921, BJ446, BS730 and BS796.

and attacked. Flight Lieutenant Cecil Courtney-Clarke and F/Sgt 'Rod' Lawrence were in a good position to fire at the bomber, a Ki-21, and neutralised the rear gunner after he had fired one burst. The bomber disappeared into cloud, but was losing height with one engine smoking. Therefore, it could only be claimed as a probable. The rest of the month consisted of three raids on the 25th, 26th and 28th and ended with escorts for Blenheims on the 30th and 31st. The results for the month were pretty good for the Mohawk, a type regarded as totally obsolete by 1943. That month, the squadron recorded 287 operational flying hours out of a total of 375. February was more intense (136 sorties flown) with escorts, Rhubarbs and several scrambles. All but one of these scrambles involved friendly aircraft. On the 12th, however, Flight Sergeants Derek Wicks and William Garnett took off from the forward airfield near Maungdaw on their own initiative upon learning of Japanese aircraft in the area. They had just identified an 'Army O1', actually Ki-43s, when Wicks felt strikes on his aircraft from behind and took violent evasive action. A series of dogfights then took place. Wicks got on the tail of one Ki-43 that dived away. He followed it down firing repeatedly from close range. When the Ki-43 was almost at tree top height, and Wicks was about to break away, he was attacked from astern by another enemy aircraft and so lost sight of the first one. It did not re-appear and he believed that it had crashed, confirmed later by a column of smoke near the spot. The crash had also been witnessed from the ground. So far the squadron had been in a rich vein of luck, with no losses to report. That came to an end on the 18th when F/Sgt Morgan was posted missing during a non-operational flight in AR650, but fortunately he was reported safe the next day. The same day, F/O Tovey was killed while conducting a flight test near Agartala aerodrome. He was seen to spin into the ground. Two days later, on the 21st, changes occurred regarding the flight commanders with both being replaced. Flying Officer J. Rashleigh took over B Flight while F/L Courtney-Clarke replaced F/L David Cunliffe at the head of A Flight.

The first week of March was quiet and the pilots saw little activity. The first large scale operation of the month was mounted on the 7th with an escort for Blenheims. The squadron provided twelve Mohawks for the task, led by the wing leader, S/L Pitt-Brown. However, this number was reduced enroute because of bad weather and only five could continue to the target while the others, separated from the main formation, had to divert to Dohazari. The next day, a new CO, S/L Guy J.C. Hogan, took over the unit. Over the next two days, the squadron was called upon to provide more escorts to Blenheims, but returned to close support work on the 12th when four Mohawks, each carrying six 40-lb bombs, accompanied three Hudsons on a supply dropping mission, while four other Mohawks acted as top cover. The Mohawks returned to the usual escort duty for the next few days and were even selected to provide escort to the first raid by RAF Vultee Vengeances on 19 March.

One could be surprised in the selection of an aircraft totally obsolete in 1943, but the Mohawk had an advantage over the Hurricane in that it was much more manoeuvrable and could therefore tangle with the Ki-43 better than the Hurricane could. Escorts of bombers or transport aircraft would be the main task of the squadron until the end of the month, but, on the 29th in the afternoon, six Mohawks were scrambled, together with Hurricanes of Nos. 79 and 135 Squadrons when hostile aircraft were reported approaching. Over Maungdaw, twelve Ki-43s were seen at 16,000 feet when the Mohawks were heading south 1,000 feet higher. Nine of the Japanese were to their left and three to the right. The British pilots peeled off to attack the former group and a confused dogfight commenced. At the end, P/O William Lee claimed one Ki-43 probable and two more damaged. On the negative side, the engine of F/O 'Dizzy' Mendizabal's Mohawk (coded 'O') seized and he had to make a belly-landing about twenty miles north of base. Next morning, four Mohawks led by S/L Hogan, were airborne at 08.30 to intercept hostile aircraft to the south. They were ordered to Maungdaw at 15,000 feet and then vectored 300 degrees. At that time, radio contact was lost and soon after bombs were seen bursting over Hove. Hogan therefore decided to bring back his aircraft east to base. Here, six Ki-43s were spotted between 10,000 and 12,000 feet. Hogan gave the order to attack. A general dogfight then began and F/O 'Paddy' Chancellor got a good burst at one which fell away in a steep dive. He claimed it as a probable while claims were also made by S/L Hogan and F/O B. Snowball for one damaged aircraft each (i.e. 5 Sqn ORB). However, F/L J. Rasleigh (in Mohawk 'S') found his windscreen covered in oil and was then shot-up. His rudder controls were shot away and one aileron was rendered inoperable. Smoke began to appear in the cockpit. He had no choice but to crash-land near Kanakapura in a small clearing, but, as the flaps were ineffective, his landing speed was 140mph. He could not avoid cows in the clearing and killed three of them before the aircraft stopped, the engine torn away. Amazingly, he was uninjured. The next day, the squadron was airborne again for further interceptions but all was quiet. The month ended with more 200 sorties and 625 operational hours flown. The Mohawks flown by Mendizabal and Rasleigh were not a total loss and were salvaged but as they were repaired or not is not known.

The first days of April were busy. On the 1st, led by the CO, seven Mohawks were airborne for a sweep in conjunction with Hurricanes of Nos. 135 and 136 Squadrons and, the following day, six Mohawks served as top cover for Hurricanes attacking enemy vessels in the morning. In the afternoon, a sweep of six aircraft was mounted. The next day, the same tasks. An escort in the morning and a fighter sweep in the afternoon. Operations continued almost daily until the 23rd. No further sorties were carried out after that date. On the 6th, the Japanese bombed Argatala causing some damage on the ground but none to the squadron. Nobody was able to get airborne in time to intercept. Some more interceptions were carried out in the next few days, but all were uneventful. Twelve days later, while attacking Japanese troop concentrations in a rest camp near Alethangyaw, F/L Chancellor (RNZAF) was seen to hit the ground with his guns still firing. It is believed that he misjudged the height and possibly became fixated on the target. Chancellor was actually from Northern Ireland who had lived in Australia and New Zealand before the war. When he tried to enlist in the RAF in London, the waiting lists were too long so he decided to return to New Zealand and enlist in the RNZAF. To confirm how busy April was, at the end of month the squadron could be proud of close to 500 hours flown, 350 on operations, in 180 sorties.

Only training flights were carried out in the first days of May with an interesting challenge on the 4th when a Mosquito came face to face with a Mohawk in flight. Of course, the pilot of Mosquito could do what he wanted but the Mohawk was still unbeatable in the turn. New NCO pilots were posted in and, despite the announcement of a pending re-equipment with new aircraft, the pilots had to receive basic training and minor accidents continued to occur. For example, on 10 May the landing gear of AR690, returning from a training flight, collapsed, but without major consequence for the pilot nor the aircraft. The aircraft was eventually struck off charge on 1 March 1944. Victims of another accident that month, BB925 on the 20th and BS731 on the 24th, both were struck off charge at the same time as AR690. On the operational side, the squadron was airborne, early in the morning of the 6th, from Reindeer, where it was on detachment, to attack Japanese positions on a ridge. The six Mohawks were each armed with ten 20-lb bombs. The raid was led by F/L Rashleigh, all returned safely to base, and later received confirmation from British ground personnel that the attack had been successful. It was a busy day as another raid was carried out and an interception patrol was also flown just before this raid that took place late in the afternoon. Two days later, other ground support ops were flown as well as an attempt to intercept an enemy aircraft. The squadron remained busy until the 24th when all operational flying ceased. The Squadron had received notice on the 16th that it was to move to Kharagpur to be re-equipped with Hurricanes. The operation was led by the CO from Reindeer to bomb Japanese positions once more. That month, about 100 sorties were achieved for a total of 315 operational hours in 410 hours flown. Close to 65,000 rounds were fired and 500 20-lb bombs dropped. The association with the Mohawk came to an end and the aircraft seem to have been left at Argatala where 155 Squadron was about to arrive. No further flights were undertaken on Mohawks at Kharagpur (and no flights at all between 1 and 13 June) with all flying recorded there being on Hurricanes.

## Claims - 5 Squadron (Confirmed and Probable)

| *Date* | *Pilot* | *SN* | *Origin* | *Type* | *Serial* | *Code* | *Nb* | *Cat.* |
|---|---|---|---|---|---|---|---|---|
| **20.08.42** | Sgt William S.S. **Garnett** | RAF No. 904200 | RAF | Ki-36 | | | 1.0 | C |
| **07.10.42** | F/Sgt Roderick R. **Lawrence** | Can./ R.59882 | RCAF | Ki-48 | **BB925** | R | 1.0 | C |
| **10.11.42** | Sgt Francis A. **Gore** | RAF No. 771939 | RAF | Ki-43 | | | 1.0 | P |
| | P/O Richard S. **Tovey** | RAF No. 111323 | RAF | Ki-43 | | | 1.0 | C |
| | S/L Wiliam **Pitt-Brown** | RAF No. 33348 | RAF | Ki-43 | | | 1.0 | C |
| **19.01.43** | F/L David O. **Cunliffe** | RAF No. 87639 | RAF | Ki-43 | | | 1.0 | P |
| | F/O Arthur S. **Boyes** [1] | RAF No. 119706 | RAF | Ki-43 | **AR681** | S | 1.0 | C* |
| **22.01.43** | F/L Cecil S. **Courtney-Clarke** | RAF No. 42335 | RAF | Ki-21 | | | 0.5 | P |
| | F/Sgt Roderick R. **Lawrence** | Can./ R.59882 | RCAF | | **BB925** | R | 0.5 | P |
| **12.02.43** | F/Sgt Derek R. **Wicks** | RAF No. 929948 | RAF | Ki-43 | | D | 1.0 | C |
| **29.03.43** | P/O William J.N. **Lee** | RAF No. 112434 | RAF | Ki-43 | **BJ439** | V | 1.0 | P |
| **30.03.43** | F/O Robert N. **Chancellor** | NZ411859 | (UK)/RNZAF | Ki-43 | | R | 1.0 | P |

***Total: 11.0***

*[1] From Brazil of British parentage*

**by collision*

## Summary of the aircraft lost on Operations - 5 Squadron

| Date | Pilot | S/N | Origin | Serial | Code | Fate |
|---|---|---|---|---|---|---|
| **18.05.42** | F/Sgt Robert D. **Cameron** | RAF No. 776154 | RAF | **BJ542** | | † |
| **24.05.42** | Sgt Alan T. **Wood** | RAF No. 785063 | RAF | **AR676** | | † |
| | F/Sgt Christopher G. **Campbell** | RAF No. 1001167 | RAF | **BJ546** | OQ-O | † |
| **30.09.42** | F/Sgt William G. **Thomas** | RAF No. 655553 | RAF | **AX695** | | † |
| **07.10.42** | W/O Ewen R. **Worts** | NZ405357 | RNZAF | **BB974** | | - |
| **15.01.43** | F/O Peter M. **Bellinger** | RAF No. 108238 | RAF | **BK572** | N | **PoW** |
| **19.01.43** | F/O Arthur S. **Boyes** [1] | RAF No. 119706 | RAF | **AR681** | S | - |
| **18.04.43** | F/O Robert N. **Chancellor** | NZ411859 | (UK)/RNZAF | **BS790** | | † |

***Total: 8***

*[1] From Brazil of British parentage*

Two more Canadians of 5 Sqn in 1943: P/O Harold O. Seifert (on the wing) and P/O Rodolfo Mendizabal. Note the maple leaf painted on the nose of the Mohawk. Both would be killed flying Hurricanes, still with 5 Sqn, before the year was over.

## Summary of the aircraft lost by accident - 5 Squadron

| Date | Pilot | S/N | Origin | Serial | Code | Fate |
|---|---|---|---|---|---|---|
| **18.01.42** | F/L Eric C. **Fyson** | RAF No. 40103 | RAF | **BJ438** | | - |
| **03.04.42** | Sgt Charles T. **Kronk** | NZ41514 | RNZAF | **AR678** | | - |
| **25.04.42** | W/C Harbourne M. **Stephen** | RAF No. 78851 | RAF | **AR644** | | - |
| **17.05.42** | P/O Jonathan **Rasleigh** | RAF No. 108462 | RAF | **BS786** | Z | - |
| **19.06.42** | P/O Thomas J. **Trimble** | Can./ J.7442 | RCAF | **AR641** | | - |
| | F/Sgt Errol W.J. **Blake** | RAF No. 785051 | (IRE)/RAF | **BJ534** | M | † |
| **03.10.42** | Sgt Percy T. **Cutfield** | NZ404903 | RNZAF | **BS735** | | - |
| **24.11.42** | Sgt Thomas G. **Smith** | RAF No. 629168 | RAF | **BJ446** | | - |
| **18.02.43** | Sgt Peter **Morgan** | RAF No. 1194249 | RAF | **AR650** | | - |
| **19.02.43** | P/O Richard S. **Tovey** | RAF No. 111323 | RAF | **BB977** | D | † |

***Total: 10***

Mohawks of 5 Sqn in flight; BJ439/V leading 'S' and two others. Unusually, it seems that the 'V' was painted in red. *(Andrew Thomas)*

# August 1942
# January 1944

**Victories - confirmed or probable claims: 6.50**

**First operational sortie:**
**20.09.42**
**Last operational sortie:**
**29.12.43**

**Number of sorties:** *ca.***900**

**Total aircraft written-off: 17**

Aircraft lost on operations: 13
Aircraft lost in accidents: 4

## Squadron code letters:

**-**

### Commanding Officers

| | | | | |
|---|---|---|---|---|
| S/L Donald W.A. Stones | RAF No. 42276 | RAF | ... | 01.11.42 |
| S/L Charles G. St.D. Jeffries | RAF No. 41929 | RAF | 01.11.42 | 13.11.43 |
| S/L Dennis Winton | RAF No. 88722 | RAF | 13.11.43 | ... |

# Squadron Usage

Number 155 Squadron was formed on 1 April 1942 at Peshawar. Command was given to Squadron Leader 'Don' Stones who brilliantly served with 79 Squadron in May-June 1940, and during the Battle of Britain, before serving at Malta and then the Far East. An ace with a DFC and Bar, he had been B Flight Commander at No. 67 Squadron flying Hurricanes. No aircraft were available at the time of formation and the squadron had to wait until the first days of August to see the first Mohawks arrive. In July the squadron moved to St. Thomas Mount (Madras). The delays were caused by technical changes to the aircraft. Modifications comprised a British turn and bank

'Porky' Jeffries joined the RAF before the war and made his initial claims in France in May 1940 with 3 Sqn. He later participated in the early stages of the Battle of Britain before sailing to Malta where he would make the bulk of his claims. Following the end of his tour and a rest, he was posted to the Far East where he took over 155, his last operational posting of the war. He ended the war with a DFC and Bar and continued to serve in the peacetime RAF.

The Mohawk in which 'Porky' Jeffries made his only claim on the type, BB928, on 28 January 1943. Note the squadron leader pennant painted on the cowling, an unusual location, the personal markings behind the cowling and the victory markings under the cockpit (see colour profile). Note that no individual letter appears here on BB928, normally it was Z. However, its size and the exact location forward the roundel are not known. It is believed that the aircraft was probably being receiving a new paint as suggests the absence of the yellow in the fuselage roundel. (see colour profile) *(BS Wapiti via P. Sortehaug)*

indicator and artificial horizons and changing the position of the electrical switch for undercarriage and flaps from the side of the cockpit to a more convenient and accessible position on the control column. In the meantime, some flights were undertaken on Hurricanes while awaiting collection of the Mohawks. At last, the first batch of six Mohawks arrived from the MU led by F/L Peter Rathie who had fought over Malta the previous year. A second batch of five Mohawks followed on the 26th led by the CO. Training had begun in the meantime. More machines arrived on 1 September and conversions proceeded quickly. On 20 September, the squadron performed its first two convoy patrols and, the same day, the last Mohawks were taken on charge, bringing the number in the squadron to twenty. On 25 September, A Flight, under the command of F/L Rathie, was detailed to proceed to Vizagapatam and, between the 27th and 30th, eight reconnaissance and convoy patrols were carried out with each lasting two hours. Those patrols of two aircraft were flown again on 1 October. The main event in October, however, was the preparation to move to Alipore (Jessore) which took place on the 18th. A sector reconnaissance was flown from there on the 25th. The squadron was now ready for action and, on the 30th, eleven aircraft carried out an attack on Shwebo aerodrome. All aircraft returned safely to base.

Two Mohawks of 155 Sqn flying over the Indian mountains in 1942. Mohawk 'B' was normally BJ451.

'Tom' Buddle was a New Zealander who joined the Straits Settlement Volunteer Air Force at Singapore in February 1941. In May 1942, he was one of the first pilot to join No. 155 Squadron in formation. He would to remain with the squadron two years until May 1944 when he was posted to the Middle East to serve as an instructor at No. 73 OTU. By that time he had been awarded the DFC in December 1943 and transferred to the RNZAF (since January).
*(Mrs J. Buddle via P. Sortehaug)*

On 1 November 1942, S/L Stones left the squadron and command was temporarily given to F/L Rathie until the new CO arrived. Eight days later, four Mohawks piloted by F/L Rathie, F/O H.A Nicholson, P/O D.A. Allen and Sgt J.A. Simpson were detailed to proceed to Koladan River and beat up river craft carrying Japanese supplies. On the 10th, the unit was called upon to escort eight Blenheims from Nos. 60 and 113 Squadrons to Akyab. The escort was led by F/L Rathie. The formation was caught by Ki-43s from the 64th Sentai. Before any action could be taken by the British, two pilots were shot down in quick succession. Flying Officer John Squibb and P/O Roy McClumpha were both posted as missing believed killed. In the ensuing combat, however, the squadron had its revenge and P/O 'Tom' Buddle (a New Zealander serving in the RAF) and F/L Rathie each claimed one Ki-43 destroyed. Rathie's claim was shared with a Blenheim gunner from 113 Squadron. On 24 November, the squadron moved to Agartala, east of Dacca.

In December, with the new wing formed (No. 169), the squadron began to practice with the other Mohawk unit, No. 5 Squadron. On the 5th, six aircraft led by F/L Rathie went to Chittagong for readiness duties. They continuously scrambled after reconnaissance aircraft during the day but always arrived too late to make an interception. At 15.30, they were scrambled again, but this time it was to intercept a raid of 25 Japanese bombers escorted by about fifty fighters. The Mohawks were caught by Ki-43s before they could get in a good position to attack the bombers and the aircraft flown by P/O Anthony Dunford was severely damaged. Dunford ultimately made a forced landing, sustaining wounds in the process that required a stay in hospital. Rathie came to the rescue of Dunford and shot the Japanese aircraft down. In the same combat, another Ki-43 was claimed as damaged (F/O W.B. McGregor). Over the next four days, further scrambles were carried out but no interceptions were made. Until the end of the month, the squadron carried out various duties, from escort to ground attack, with no loss. From the 12th, the ops were led by the new CO, S/L 'Porkie' Jeffries DFC. Jefferies had flown in the Battle of France and Battle of Britain who had served in Malta before being posted to the Far East.

New Year's Day 1943 started in the worst way for the squadron. The CO, with his wingman, P/O Allan Haley (RAAF), took off for a strafing sortie over the Chindwin River. The Japanese AA fire was intense and Haley's Mohawk was hit. He was posted missing believed killed. During the month, the squadron provided escort to Blenheims a couple of times but the main task remained ground strafing. Two more Mohawks were lost on the 14th when F/Sgt George Potter (a New Zealander serving in the RAF) in AX893 and Sgt Adam Boult in BT471 collided while escorting Blenheims to Magwe. Both pilots were killed. Their bodies were found the next day in the wreckage. Duties were carried out as usual and, in all, about thirty sorties were recorded. Despite this low number of sorties and the loss of two pilots and machines, a third pilot would be lost on the 28th. That day, the squadron was tasked with escorting Blenheims. Flight

Mohawk AR656/X seen at dispersal late in 1942. Number 155 Squadron painted the individual letter ahead of the roundel in white. This was found to be enough to distinguish its aircraft from those of 5 Sqn. AR656 was to be struck of charge on 29 February 1944.
*(Andrew Thomas)*

Lieutenant D. Winton led the three Mohawks. One suffered an engine failure in flight and F/O Derek Allen chose to bail out. He was seen to land safely but was never seen again. Later that day, the CO and three other pilots undertook a sweep to Akyab Island as part of 169 Wing operations. Squadron Leader Jeffries was at 14,000 feet when he saw a Ki-43 diving at high speed and apparently trailing smoke, right through the formation. He gave it a good burst at 70 yards and it continued diving. Initially claimed as damaged it would be later confirmed as destroyed by group following a report of a Japanese pilot seen to bale out.

During the first days of February, another move occurred with the squadron going to Rajyeswarpur. It would remain there, with some detachments to Imphal, for the entire month before moving to Imphal where it would remain until July. Air operations in February were limited and consisted mainly of some armed-reconnaissances carried out with a limited number of aircraft during which some ground targets were strafed. Some Mohawks were hit by AA at various times, but each time they were able to return to base for repair.

While based at Imphal, the rhythm of operations increased significantly. On the 4th, F/L Rathie led a formation of seven Mohawks in support of the Army. Intense AA was encountered but none of the aircraft were hit. Mainly called upon for ground attack, the squadron also provided escorts for photo-reconnaissance Hurricanes which were in high demand by the Army. When not required for specific missions, the squadron carried out offensive patrols.

Operations continued in April and, for the first time, the squadron exceeded 100 sorties in a month. On the 15th, the CO led three other pilots to escort a Hudson on a supply mission. The four Mohawks returned without anything to report, but it seems that one of the pilots made a heavy landing in BJ544. The Mohawk was first declared as Category 'B' but was later reclassified as 'E' and struck off charge on 29 February 1944. It seems that no repairs were carried out to return it to flying condition. On the 20th, the routine was changed when the squadron scrambled in the afternoon to intercept a Japanese raid spotted at 20,000 feet. The Japanese formation consisted of eighteen bombers escorted by 24 fighters flying 4,000 feet above them. Only two sections of Mohawks arrived in time to attack. Flight Lieutenant Rathie and F/O MacGregor each claimed one Ki-21 damaged. They could not go further with their attacks as the escort soon interfered. Rathie escaped but he saw MacGregor in combat with five or six fighters and Rathie then got in to a good position to shoot at one of the Ki-43s, which was hit in the engine and cockpit, which was claimed as a probable. MacGregor, meanwhile, dived steeply onto another, seeing hits and then seeing the aircraft go into a spin from 3,000 feet. MacGergor claimed this one as probable too. This engagement seems to favour the Mohawks, but it did not as the Japanese shot down two Mohawks. Flight Sergeant James A. Simpson, Rathie's wingman, and F/Sgt Hubert T. Freeman (RAAF), flying as MacGregor's wingman, were both killed. Both had been separated from their leaders during the combat. Simpson's body was found two days later but Freeman would never be found.

The next day, the Japanese returned to Imphal to bomb the aerodrome and, once again, 155 was ordered off with eight Mohawks led by the CO. They were able to get in to position at 27,000 feet, above the Japanese bomber and fighters (respectively flying at 22,000 and 26,000 feet). Before the Mohawks could attack, the bombers dropped their bombs and disappeared in a shallow dive. The Ki-43s, however, turned back and engaged the Mohawks. Squadron Leader Jefferies and F/O Hunter found eight of them at 23,000 feet apparently serving as decoys while eight more stayed above as top cover. The two British pilots singled out one of the higher formation and attacked them from 26,000 feet, but the ensuing combat did not produce any results other than the two Mohawks were eventually separated from the rest of the formation. Flight Sergeant Christison developed engine trouble and was obliged to make a wheels down forced landing. Flying Officer Weir was left alone and had to face two Japanese who shot him up but he managed to land without incident. The four other Mohawks engaged too but only F/O Meyer claiming one Ki-43 damaged. The remaining Mohawks returned to base with no further claims or losses to report. After those two intensive days, the squadron finished the month off by flying various ground attack sorties and escorting Dakota transports.

In May, the unit carried out around seventy sorties during which 70,500 rounds were fired, 124 20-lb and 24 40-lb bombs were dropped and 230 hours were flown. On the 4th, returning from a *Rhubarb* sortie, the engine of the Mohawk (BK580) flown by F/S R. Bugge developed a serious oil leak obliging the pilot to make an exceptional (as per the CO) forced landing at Dimapur. The Mohawk was slightly damaged and put in Category 'B' but nothing is known about its subsequent use. Some sources give it as lost that day, but as it

Mohawk BJ442/Y being prepared for another flight. Note the position of the letter 'Y' just under the cockpit, unusual for an RAF fighter, but common for 155 Sqn. *(Andrew Thomas)*

Two 155 Sqn Mohawks at dispersal early in 1943. In the foreground is Mohawk 'W', possibly BS795. Note the position of the individual letter, like BJ442/Y (see previous page), under the cockpit. *(Andrew Thomas)*

was eventually SOC on 1 March 1944, it is thought that it was repaired and possibly returned to the squadron. The biggest raid of the month occurred on the last day of May when an important bridge in the Kalyemo area was attacked and destroyed by the squadron. Four raids were needed to obtain the results, with 18,150 rounds fired and sixty 20-lb and 24 40-lb bombs dropped.

On 1 June 1943, F/O Brinnand (Southern Rhodesia) and F/O MacGregor took off at 15.34 for a *Rhubarb* sortie around the Kalyemo area and the target was strafed and silenced. Flying Officer Brinnand's Mohawk was hit by two bullets and he was forced to make an emergency landing. He was seen to set fire to the aircraft and walk off westwards. He would make contact with British forces nine days later and returned to the squadron soon afterwards. The rest of the month's flying was concentrated in the Kaltemo area which led to the use of 46,500 rounds of ammunition and the dropping of 200 bombs including 112 forty pounders in about sixty offensive sorties. This routine was regularly challenged by scrambles (about ten or so) that all proved to be unsuccessful (13th and 16th). The last four days of June were not suitable for flying and at the end of the month the squadron returned to its old base of Agartala to sit out the worst of

Engine of BS736/P being warmed-up before another flight. Two mechanics are seated on the tail to prevent it from lifting. Note the wingtips and the mainwheel leg fairing painted in yellow as quick identification markings.

the monsoon. Until 10 September, when 155 returned to Imphal, the monsoon prevented much flying. Altogether, only eighty sorties were carried out. While no operational losses were recorded, the squadron lost BS795 during a training flight on 23 July. The engine caused trouble and F/O 'Tom' Buddle tried to make a forced landing back at base. The Mohawk swung on landing and the undercarriage collapsed. It was categorised 'B' but the decision was made not to carry out any repairs. The type was at the end of its career with the RAF and enough airframes were still available as 155 was now the only RAF squadron flying the Mohawk. BS795 was therefore struck off charge on 31 December. It is believed that BS734 met the same fate when it was the victim of a taxiing accident on 3 August. The pilot, Sgt A.J.F. Parish escaped injury. The accident occurred during the pilot's first solo on type and, due to the inexperience of the pilot, the Mohawk ended up in a drainage ditch, sustaining Category 'B' damage.

The squadron began its move to Imphal on 2 September. This was completed on the 10th. There, it was noticed that the runway surface was very rough, and was cutting the tyres of the aircraft, so, to prevent any accidents, the aircraft were grounded for a while. Repairs to the runway took a week. The next day, the 20th, the squadron returned to operations with a *Rhubarb* mission led by S/L Jefferies. Thirty-five 20-lb and thirty 40-lb bombs were dropped and targets widely strafed with 8,100 rounds fired. Aside from the operational flights, the squadron was now responsible for training new pilots as no further courses were available for hopeful Mohawk pilots. The same day, Sgt W.G. Wolsteholme took AR646 for a first solo and, returning from this first flight, it seems the landing was a bit rough and the undercarriage collapsed. The Mohawk was only good for scrap and components which was somewhat fortunate knowing that spare parts were not easy to find out at that time. The CO led the following raid on the 24th with the next one on the 29th led by F/L Ford who also led the two ops carried out the 30th, the last one being an unsuccessful interception. The squadron was properly back on operations in October as more than 140 sorties were flown in 25 days. On the 4th, four aircraft led by F/L Ford took off at 08.43 for an interception under the control of the Fighter Operations Room. While the interception was a non-event, F/Sgt Barrett Christison force landed at Cox's Bazaar following engine trouble and the aircraft was damaged enough not to consider any repairs and the aircraft was struck off charge four days later. Despite the high number of ops, nothing happened until the 28th. The squadron carried out three strikes in the afternoon and during the third F/Sgt Bugge's engine, on the return leg, began to falter although it was not believed to be as a result of ground fire as no AA was encountered. He was obliged to make a forced landing three miles from Sibong. Bugge was injured dying of his wounds later in the day and the Mohawk was a total write-off. While the type was at the end of its career, the Mohawk had been intensively used despite its age and obsolescence. The squadron had fired an impressive 131,380 rounds of ammunition and dropped close to 23,000 pounds of bombs, including some 30-lb incendiaries.

In November, 155 continued its close air support for the Army, but on the 9th, it reverted to the fighter role for the first time since April. The day started with a 'Dinah' spotted flying at 27,000 feet. Flying Officer Buddle and F/Sgt Pinch, who were on readiness, took off under control of the No. 9 Fighter Operations Room in Imphal. They climbed as quickly as the old machines could and were able to get as close as half mile from the 'Dinah'. As soon as the two Mohawks were seen, the Japanese pilot increased speed and turned back to

Three Mohawks of 155 Sqn flying in formation (the third is visible flying well below). In the foreground is AR674/H. Note the red in the national markings has now been deleted. The Mohawk behind still has its fuselage roundel outlined in yellow. *(LT Hunter via Paul Sortehaug)*

friendly lines. The Mohawks simply could not follow it despite having an advantage of altitude! The flight was a success, however, as the two Mohawks forced the reconnaissance aircraft to end its mission prematurely. For the fighter pilots, though, the frustration was intense. Half an hour later, another 'Dinah' was spotted. Two Mohawks flown by F/O MacGregor and Sgt McCormick took off and the same thing happened. At the end of the morning, everything that the squadron could scramble, ten Mohawks, raced to get airborne. Two enemy formations of sixteen 'Sally' bombers and six 'Oscars' each were inbound. One formation attacked the Imphal strip while the other bombed Palel strip. Two Mohawks intercepted two Ki-43s and, in the ensuing combat, F/L Dunford in BS798/V claimed one Ki-43 destroyed which was seen to crash ten miles north-east of Palel. The other Mohawks also saw combat, but no claims or losses were made, even though the Mohawk flown by Sgt Tester (BT470/F) was damaged. Dunford's claim would be the last one made by a Mohawk pilot. In all, 3,000 rounds were fired during that encounter. It is worth noting that the Hurricanes based at Palel were also called to intercept and on returning to base it soon became clear that, during combat, it was easy to confuse an Oscar with a Mohawk. To prevent any dramatic mistake in the future, it was decided to paint the lower half of the Mohawks' engine cowlings yellow. The Japanese were back two days later, but 155 did not intercept. The next day, the squadron carried out a strike on villages occupied by the Japanese, but one aircraft (BB975) had to return to base early with engine trouble and its undercarriage collapsed on landing at Imphal. The aircraft was not repaired and would be struck off charge on 29 February. The strike, led by F/L Meredith, was considered successful. The following day, on the 13th, S/L Jefferies handed over the squadron to S/L Dennis Winton. Winton was not a newcomer as he had previously served as a flight commander before leaving for a rest period. That day, various ground attack ops were carried out and, shortly after midday, F/L Bruce M. Ross-Margenty, from New Delhi, took off to lead three other aircraft on a strike. While taking off, a couple of bombs fell off and exploded before the pilot could achieve a safe height. Ross-Margenty was killed instantly. The rest of the month was uneventfully split between offensive strikes and some unsuccessful interceptions. It must be mentioned that the squadron was now facing a serviceability problem with the average of number of Mohawks available during the month being nine aircraft and the total strength did not exceed thirteen aircraft (the normal complement was sixteen). Only the number of pilots was right, 25, with three new pilots arriving that month.

In December, the squadron returned to ground attack duties while some training or test flights were also carried out, mainly by the new pilots. During one such flight, BB921 crashed on take off for an air test on the 12th shortly after the aircraft was delivered to the squadron. The pilot, Sgt W.F. Tester, came to no harm. Another Mohawk was also lost on Christmas Day, on landing this time, but the identity of the pilot could not be traced. The squadron only flew operationally that day. In both cases, the Mohawk was categorised as Cat.B damage, but repairs were later judged unnecessary as the type was now about to be withdrawn from use. On 29 December, S/L Winton took off at 10.00 at the head of six Mohawks to bomb and strafe Japanese positions at Yazagyo. That was the squadron's last op on Mohawks and, therefore, the last sorties by RAF Mohawks. In December, the squadron had flown seventy sorties.

In January, 155 began to prepare for the move to Alipore to be converted to Spitfire Mk. VIIIs. This was done on the 4th and the first Spitfire flights took place on the 6th. That same day, all of the Mohawks were sent to the Maintenance Units for final disposal. The war of the Mohawk was over.

This Mohawk was usually flown by F/O 'Tim' Meyer and is seen in the type's final colour scheme before its withdrawal, although the cowling undersurfaces do not seem to be painted in yellow meaning that the photo would have been taken before 9 November (see text). Meyer used to name his aircraft 'Joe Soap', so here is 'Joe Soap II'. This aircraft is often said to be BS734, but it is not certain (see photo next page).
'Tim' Meyer would later command 615 Sqn, flying Spitfires, at the end of war.

Combat report:
A.B. Dunford, 9 November 1943

APP C

From:- No. 155 Squadron, R.A.F. **SECRET.**

255

To:- Air Headquarters, India (2)
Air Headquarters, Bengal.
Headquarters, No.221 Group.
No. 170 Wing Ops.

Date:- 10th. November 1943.

Ref:- 155S/S.1862/1/Int.

**Report By F/O.DUNFORD. Claiming Destruction Of 1 ARMY 01.**

Flying Mohawk 4 - V 677, (Call Sign Green 1) together with F/O. Edwards in Q'(Call Sign Green 2) I was airborne at Imphal 1140 Hours. As pre-arranged we headed North for KANGLETOMBI, gaining height as quickly as possible. At about 9,000ft.I picked up a message from the Controller to 'Blue Leader' saying 'Bandits 20 Miles East Of Base' following which I immediately turned West, still gaining height. At 11,000ft. I saw 2 other Mohawks on my Port Beam, so turned to join up with them. On joining up we turned South and saw H.A.A. bursts over the Aerodrome and approx 16 T/E Aircraft apparently bombing the Area. All 4 of us then turned East in an attempt to cut off the Bombers on their homeward track, at the same time avoiding the Imphal Gun Zone. Shortly after this I saw another formation of approx the same number of T/E Aircraft flying South 15 Miles away from us and approx 10 miles S.of PALEL. Realising the impossibility of catching this formation we ignored them and continued our pursuit of the first formation who by now were travelling S.E. away from Imphal at a high speed. Our 2 Sections then parted company, mine climbing to gain more height. At approx 10 Miles East of Palel I saw what appeared to be 4 Radial-Engined Aircraft. Assuming they were Mohawks, I turned to join up with them, approaching them I suddenly saw them break in a manner that indicated to me that one pair was enemy. By that time I was flying at 19,000ft,approximately 4,000ft, above the 4 Aircraft, 1 of these turned to starboard and I positively identified it as an 01 by the roundels on its wings. I saw that it was on the tail of a Mohawk rapidly closing in. I looked round and seeing no other enemy I called to my No.2 'Look Out' 9 o'clock, Going In Now'. I dived down onto the 01 giving him a 3 second burst deflection shot from the quarter position above. He immediately ceased chasing the Mohawk and pulled round in a steep climbing turn to Starboard. I followed him round giving him continuous bursts, still from the quarter position above. He then dived down vertically and I turned over on my back to follow him. He soon pulled out of his dive and straightened up. I also straightened up and came astern of him at about 500 yards. I gave full throttle in attempt to close the range, but was only overtaking him very slowly. I opened fire with a 6 second burst at about 300 yards observing dewild strikes along his wings. He took no evasive action whatever and I gave him another 7 to 9 second burst, again observing strikes. He went into a rate 1 turn to Starboard, and I gave him another 3 second burst from the fine quarter following which he momentarily straightened up, then turned on his back and dived vertically, smoke streaming from his engine. I looked round again and seeing no Aircraft following me, I followed him down and on pressing the trigger to give him a final burst, I found my guns empty. Although at that time I was travelling at over 300 miles per hour I was unable to close the range andhe dissapeared from my view. I continued on in Aileron turns to approx 4,000ft. No other Aircraft in the vicinity, I returned to Base and landed at 1235 hours. F/O.BISHOP flying B.798 the Mohawk mentioned as being attacked in this report confirms seeing the 01 crash into the ground and explode after diving away from me. I therefore claim the destruction of that Aircraft.

(Signed) A.B. DUNFORD.--------F/O.

## Claims - 155 Squadron (Confirmed and Probable)

| Date | Pilot | SN | Origin | Type | Serial | Code | Nb | Cat. |
|---|---|---|---|---|---|---|---|---|
| **08.11.42** | F/O Thomas J. **BUDDLE** | RAF No. 112430 | (NZ)/RAF | Ki-43 | | | 1.0 | C |
| | F/L Peter **RATHIE** | RAF No. 88467 | RAF | Ki-43 [1] | | | 0.5 | C |
| **05.12.42** | F/L Peter **RATHIE** | RAF No. 88467 | RAF | Ki-43 | | | 1.0 | C |
| **28.01.43** | S/L Charles G. St.D. **JEFFRIES** | RAF No. 41929 | RAF | Ki-43 | **BB928** | Z | 1.0 | C |
| **20.04.43** | F/L Peter **RATHIE** | RAF No. 88467 | RAF | Ki-43 | | | 1.0 | P |
| | F/O William B. **MCGREGOR** | RAF No. 112356 | RAF | Ki-43 | | | 1.0 | P |
| **09.11.43** | F/O Anthony B. **DUNFORD** | RAF No. 119837 | RAF | Ki-43 | **BS798** | V | 1.0 | C |

***Total: 6.50***

*[1]* shared with a Blenheim gunner from 113 Squadron

**by collision*

SECRET. 256

From:- No. 155 Squadron, R.A.F.

To:- Air Headquarters, India (2)
Air Headquarters, Bengal.
Headquarters, No.221 Group.
No. 170 Wing Ops.

Date:- 10th. November 1943.

Ref:- 155S/S.1862/Int.

REPORT BY F/O. BISHOP ON DESTRUCTION OF ARMY 01 BY F/O.DUNFORD. ON THE 9th. NOVEMBER 1943.

I was airborne in Mohawk B.798 (Call Sign Yellow 1) together with Sgt.TESTER (Yellow 2) in F.470 from Imphal at approx 1135 Hours. WE were some way behind the 3 sections which had taken off previously, we turned West and were joined by Green Se ction at about 11,000ft. We saw H.A.A. over the Aerodrome and a formation of 16 T/E Aircraft (Probably Army 97) bombing the area. We turned East between Imphal and Palel in an attempt to cut off the bombers. After turning I observed an ARMY 01 about 2,000ft above and 2 miles behind me, I warned my No.2 and climbed to attack, at this point we were attacked by 2 Hurricanes from West. I had seen them at a range of approx 1,000 yards, and suspecting they were coming in to attack me, I turned down sun to show my roundels and waggled my wings. This had no effect, they opened fire at us at approx 400 yards, closing to 150 yards. I turned steeply towards them and as they passed behind I spun. As I pulled out of the spin the 01 I had originally intended attacking dived onto me. I turned towards him and broke downwards, aileron turning. The 01 broke away and I pulled out of the dive going East. I then observed another Mohawk on the tail of the Zero 1 firing continuously. The latter turned on it's back and dived vertically into the ground, exploding as it hit it. The approx position of the crashed Enemy Fighter is within a 5 mile radius of BONGLY RK.7231 in the jungle. After the attack by the Hurricanes I was unable to see my No.2. I understand he was compelled to force-land at Palel with under-carriage and flaps down but dead engine. There were Cannon-Shell Strikes in his engine cowling and airframe.

(Signed) H.B. BISHOP. F/O.

## Summary of the aircraft lost on Operations - 155 Squadron

| Date | Pilot | S/N | Origin | Serial | Code | Fate |
|---|---|---|---|---|---|---|
| **10.11.42** | F/O John C.D. **Squibb** | RAF No. 85951 | RAF | **AX898** | | † |
| | F/O Roy C.J. **McClumpha** | RAF No. 109781 | RAF | **BB929** | | † |
| **01.01.43** | P/O Allan H. **Haley** | Aus. 402054 | RAAF | **BK584** | | † |
| **14.01.43** | F/Sgt George B. **Potter** | RAF No. 785062 | (NZ)/RAF | **AX893** | K | † |
| | F/Sgt Adam D.S. **Boult** | RAF No. 1078250 | RAF | **BT471** | H | † |
| **28.01.43** | F/O Derek A. **Allen** | RAF No. 114662 | RAF | **BT472** | N | † |
| **20.04.43** | F/Sgt James A. **Simpson** | RAF No. 946014 | RAF | **BK879** | | † |
| | F/Sgt Hubert T. **Freeman** | Aus. 404240 | RAAF | **AR653** | | † |
| **01.06.43** | F/O Jack **Brinnand** | RAF No. 80221 | (SR)/RAF | **AX889** | G | - |
| **04.10.43** | F/Sgt Barrett **Christison** | RAF No. 1311836 | RAF | **AR661** | V | - |
| **28.10.43** | F/Sgt Ronald **Bugge** | RAF No. 1294983 | RAF | **AR649** | D | † |
| **13.11.43** | F/O Bruce M. **Ross-Magenty** | RAF No. 118684 | RAF | **AR677** | W | † |
| **12.11.43** | *No details available* | ? | ? | **BB975** | | - |

***Total: 13***

Nine 155 Sqn Mohawks in flight taken shortly after the introduction of the final RAF marking style in September 1943. The aircraft seen here are BS798/B, BT470/F and AR693/D. AR661/V is behind BT470/F. Note the aircraft leading, coded 'A'. As the new SEAC roundel was officially introduced on 29 September 1943, and knowing that this aircraft was the victim of a crash-landing on 4 October, we can reasonably assume that this photo was taken between those two dates. Referring to this aircraft, coded 'A', and the previous photo featuring 'A'/Joe Soap II', we notice the difference between the roundels. They might have been changed during October, but BS734 is known to have been involved in a Cat.B accident on 3 August and there is some doubt as to whether it was repaired when the withdrawal of the type was in sight and enough Mohawks were available at MUs. Therefore, some conjecture remains as to the true identity of 'A'/'Joe Soap II' on the previous page.

Above, the same formation taken from another angle. *(LT Hunter via Paul Sortehaug)*

## Summary of the aircraft lost by accident - 155 Squadron

| *Date* | *Pilot* | *S/N* | *Origin* | *Serial* | *Code* | *Fate* |
|---|---|---|---|---|---|---|
| **23.07.43** | F/O Thomas J. **Buddle** | RAF No. 112430 | RAF | **BS795** | Y | - |
| **03.08.43** | Sgt Arthur J.F. **Parish** | RAF No. 771984 | RAF | **BS734** | A | - |
| **20.09.43** | Sgt Wilfred G.L. **Wolstenholme** | RAF No. 1336782 | RAF | **AR646** | | - |
| **12.12.43** | Sgt William F. **Tester** | RAF No. 1389315 | RAF | **BB921** | | - |

***Total: 4***

*Note: Mohawk BB920 is reported to have crashed on 25 August 1943 near Comilla after the egine seized. It is believed however that the aircraft was salvaged.*

When 169 Wing was formed with the two Mohawk squadrons, 'Bill' Pitt-Brown was chosen to become the wing leader. He used to fly BS790/WP-B with which he had claimed a Ki-43 shot down on 10 November.
*(Andrew Thomas)*

This photograph is interesting because it shows a Mohawk (even partially) with the codes 'NA' as allocated to 146 Sqn. The squadron was never fully equipped with Mohawks. Those that were allocated only remained on strength for a very short time. *(Andrew Thomas)*

# With the other units

A third fighter unit, No. 146 Squadron, used the Mohawk in small quantities. This squadron was, like many RAF units in the Far East early in the war, flying obsolete aircraft and the pilots were desperate to be re-equipped with modern fighters to replace the Hawker Audaxes recently converted into single-seat fighters. After many requests to HQ, the CO, S/L Barthold, a Battle of Britain veteran, obtained this new equipment and, on 17 March 1942, four pilots were sent to collect the aircraft (three have been identified: BB979, BS788 and BS795). The four Mohawks arrived between the 21st and 26th and training began even though the lack of a particular lubricant limited the number of flights. On 31 March, S/L Czernin, another Battle of Britain veteran, took over the squadron. The joy of receiving new aircraft was short-lived, however, as on 4 April orders were received to hand over the four Mohawks to No. 5 Squadron. All of the aircraft had left by 8 April.

In the UK, if we except the few aircraft tested by various units, the Mohawk was not widely used. The A&AEE took charge of three Mk. IIIs - AR631, AR632 and AR634 (the latter as early as 31 July 1940). One month later, AR634 was sent to storage but later on, between November 1940 and June 1941, the other two Mk. IIIs were used for various experiments and tests. From then on the aircraft saw limited use serving as unarmed communications aircraft for a couple of years with units like Nos. 24 and 510 Squadrons, the Metropolitan Communication Squadron, various Station Flights, and even No. 61 OTU. Only one was lost to an accident when it was hit on the ground on 9 March 1944. Otherwise, the Mk. III had a long career with the last one being struck off charge on 27 February 1945.

The Mk. IV was similarly tested with AR640, AR644, AR645, AR678, BK877 and, briefly, AX882 on strength with the A&AAE between August 1940 and March 1941, but not necessarily all at the same time. One was destroyed during an air raid on Boscombe Down (AR640 on 6 April 1941) while the others returned to storage for future allocation, but BK577 while used for armament tests, was lost on 1 March 1941, killing the pilot. AR644 and AR678 were eventually sent to India. AR680 was used as a communications aircraft between November 1940 and July 1941 with No. 24 Squadron before being shipped to Portugal in October, while AR636 served with Station Flight Odiham from July 1941 onwards (subsequent fate unknown). BJ438 is known to have been also used at Odiham in August 1941 before being shipped to the Far East. BJ449 were used by the RAE from 31 December 1941 onwards before it was lost in an accident on 4 February 1942 after a stall following an engine failure. The stall was provoked by misunderstanding what the ASI was reading as it was still calibrated in kph and not mph. The pilot, S/L Fiedler, was killed. Previously, the RAE had used BJ542 between December 1940 and July 1941 and would eventually later serve in India.

In the Far East, the main non-operational unit was No. 151 OTU. This unit was formed on 1 April 1942 as No. 1 OTU (India) and located at Risalpur. Its purpose was to train fighter pilots in Indian conditions for fighter and ground attack duties. It consisted of three flights: A Flight (Mohawks), B Flight (Harvards), and C Flight (Hurricanes). The first Mohawks issued to A Flight are thought to have been the former Persian aircraft (LA157-LA165), which had been assembled the previous February by Hindustan Aircraft, and AX799, the pattern aircraft for the Chinese order. The Mohawk Flight was commanded by F/L S.W. Baldie. Things did not get off to a good start when, the day after the unit's formation, LA161 suffered an engine failure, undershot on landing, and hit an obstruction. The Kiwi pilot, on his first flight in the type, escaped injuries. By June, serviceability was about five Mohawks per day when the first group of nine pilots, comprising many New Zealanders, completed their course and were posted to No. 155 Squadron. Course Number Two started soon after with twelve pupils. On 4 July, during practice aerobatics, Sgt Smith got into an inverted spin and failed to recover. He bailed out at 2,000 feet, made a successful landing about six miles out in the scrub, and returned safely to the base a couple of hours later. On 28 July, the unit became No. 151 OTU and its duties remained the same. Two days later, Sgt W. Goode had a lucky escape. During low flying practice, he flew straight into the Kabul River after the engine of LA160 lost power. He was pulled clear of the submerged aircraft by local fishermen and ferried to the bank, therefore escaping a certain death by

The few Mohawk Mk. IIIs taken on RAF charge were only used in the UK in non-operational units. Here AR633 wears the 'RG' codes of 510 Sqn, a communication unit. It was the victim of an accident on 9 March 1944 when it was hit by a Typhoon (JR509) while waiting to take-off from Milfield.

drowning. The number of Mohawks was now cut by three with only six remaining. This was soon reduced to four when two Mohawks were victims of minor accidents on 13 and 14 August. Even though the aircraft were soon repaired, their eventual return had little impact on the current course. To make-up for attrition, Mohawk DR761 built by the Hindustan Aircraft Factory was ferried from Bangalore on 30 August by F/O Murray. The type was used until the end of September when the last course, 4A (A for A Flight), completed the training. In October, more Hurricanes were taken on charge and A Flight converted over. The Mohawks from the LA and DR batches, being unsuitable for operational use, were probably put into storage as no trace of further use was found after their withdrawal from the OTU. They were probably used as spare parts sources later on and all, as far as the former Persian aircraft are concerned (batch LA), would be struck off charge in March 1944. No card seems to have survived for the former Chinese order (batch DR) but it is reasonable to think they encountered the same fate.

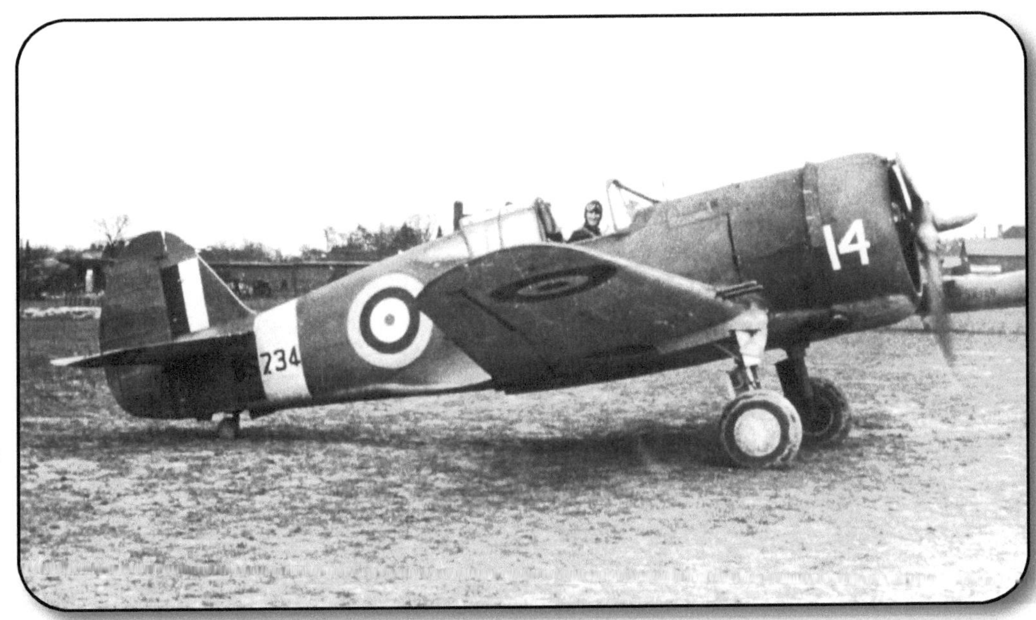


Mohawk BS734 is seen with a white '14' painted on the cowling. The aircraft behind BS734 is a Maryland, AR729, so this photograph was probably taken in UK during the winter 1940-1941. When in UK, this Mohawk was stored most of the time except in March and April 1941 where its was sent to Burtonwood where the photo was probably taken. The reason of the white '14' is unknown. Later on it served with Nos. 5 and 155 Sqns in the Far East.

Pilots photographed mid-1942, at Lower Topa, Murree Hills, on route to the Far East, before joining No. 1 (India) OTU/151 OTU.
LtoR rear: Ramsey McKelvie (UK), Basil Smith (NZ).
Front: Bill Ferguson (from Singapore), Archie Jackson (NZ), Lloyd "Babe" Hunter (NZ), Robert "Paddy" Chancellor (from Belfast, Northern Ireland), Malcolm "Mac" Edwards (NZ). At the end of their OTU, Ferguson and Chancellor would be posted to No. 5 Sqn while Hunter and Edwards to No. 155 Sqn.
*(LT Hunter via Paul Sortheaug)*

## Summary of the aircraft lost by accident - 1 (India) OTU/151 OTU

| *Date* | *Pilot* | *S/N* | *Origin* | *Serial* | *Code* | *Fate* |
|---|---|---|---|---|---|---|
| **02.04.42** | P/O Malcom H. **Edwards** | NZ411869 | RNZAF | **LA161** | | - |
| **04.07.42** | Sgt Thomas G. **Smith** | RAF No. 629168 | RAF | **LA162** | | - |
| **30.07.42** | Sgt William B. **Goode** | RAF No. 1198767 | RAF | **LA160** | | - |

***Total: 3***

Mohawk LA164 of No. 1 (India) OTU in April 1942. As far as we know, the Persian Mohawks were delivered unpainted, but for the national markings, so they were painted by the RAF with local paints which resulted in unusual shades as we can see in the photo. LA161 has received a '6' on the rudder as an individual identifier. From some personal accounts, most of the instrument panels still had their inscriptions written in Arabic. It is understood that their use came to an end, towards the end of 1942, when enough Mohawk pilots were trained. The six survivors were eventually all struck off charge on 1 March 1944.

Mohawk DR764, one of the Hindustan Aircraft Factory batch. Five are known to have been assembled before the termination of the contract (could be more) and it seems that their usefulness remained very limited because they were not totally identical to the Mohawks, coming from the French contracts, which prevented their usage by operational units. *(Andrew Thomas)*

Some Mohawks sent to the Middle East were initially used at No. 71 OTU in 1941 to train the SAAF pilots. AX888 was one of these aircraft, but was eventually handed over to the SAAF in 1943. *(Andrew Thomas)*

In the Middle East the main non-operational user was initially No. 71 OTU. Formed on 1 June 1941, at Ismailia in Egypt, its responsibilities were to train fighter and army co-operation pilots in desert conditions. This task had previously been given to No. 70 OTU. It used a great variety of aircraft including about fifteen RAF Mohawks (four of which constituted 71 OTU). The South Africans also sent some Mohawks to this unit. The first Mohawk issued was actually a SAAF aircraft, 2540, on 4 June and it was soon followed by 2544. The latter had a bad start as it was involved in a crash on the 7th suffering fuel starvation but it was ultimately repaired. The other known SAAF aircraft assigned were 2530, 2538 and 2546. In September, the unit moved to Gordon's Tree, as it was less exposed to air raids, and began to receive aircraft delivered via the Takoradi Route or Nairobi to reinforce the few SAAF airframes. With a recurrent oil system problem, serviceability remained poor by the end of 1941, about 40%, and the Mohawks were grounded a couple of times following minor accidents. Despite this, in November 1941, the Mohawk fleet flew 262 hours, and then 269 in December, with a record in January 1942 of 339. On 13 December, a fatal accident occurred when Mohawk HK823 (acquired from a deserting French pilot) collided with Tomahawk AN317. The pilot, F/L A.A.P. Weller, acting as an instructor, and who had been awarded the DFC the previous May, was killed. In the following months, the activity dropped with just 55 hours in February, 45 in March and 27 in April. In May, the OTU moved once more but the Mohawks stayed behind. Those with RAF serials are believed to have been stored and were eventually handed over to the South Africans in January and March 1943.

In November 1941, No. 73 OTU was formed near Aden with the task of training fighter pilots under desert conditions. Because personnel arrived piecemeal by sea, it officially commenced operating on 1 January 1942 with only two Mohawks and a Hurricane. On 16 April 1942, a Mohawk Flight was formed for local air defence in the wake of the attacks by the Japanese fleet on Ceylon, but it saw no action. In July 1942, the OTU reached its maximum strength of eight Mohawks, as far as the type was concerned, and in November training ceased and the unit moved to Abu Sueir in Egypt, but did not begin flying again until February 1943. Once again, however, the Mohawks were discarded. The Mohawks encountered major problems with serviceability during their presence at Aden with the fleet of eight being grounded early in August. At the end of the month, only one was available and over the following weeks it wasn't much better. The Mohawks were eventually sent to Kenya for storage and returned to SAAF authority. The Mohawks used by 73 OTU are not known, but it is possible they were all SAAF airframes. The only trace we have is in May when two SAAF Mohawks (2542 and 2549) are reported to have been victims of a minor accident meaning the SAAF contributed to the working up of this unit.

AX891 was another Mohawk in use at No. 71 OTU, wearing the number '4', Like AX888, it was to be handed to the SAAF in January 1943. *(Andrew Thomas)*

| Date | Pilot | S/N | Origin | Serial | Code | Unit | Fate |
|---|---|---|---|---|---|---|---|
| **06.04.41** | *destroyed in air raid* | - | - | **AR640** | | A&AEE | - |

Mohawks IV AR640 seen during a test flight before it was destroyed during an air raid in April 1941.

## Summary of the aircraft lost by accident - Other units

| Date | Pilot | S/N | Origin | Serial | Code | Unit | Fate |
|---|---|---|---|---|---|---|---|
| **02.01.41** | Cap M.J. **Horsey** | - | ATA | **AR658** | | 2 FPP | - |
| **08.01.41** | Sgt John M. **Gladwell** | RAF No. 740551 | RAF | **AR651** | | 8 FPP | † |
| **09.01.42** | 1st Off E.C. **Fisket** | - | ATA | **BJ445** | | 6 FPP | - |
| **14.01.41** | 1st Off E.B. **Whilden** | - | ATA | **BK579** | | 2 FPP | - |
| **01.02.41** | 1st Off F.D. **Carragher** | - | (US)/ATA | **AR664** | | 3 FPP | - |
| **01.03.41** | S/L John E. **Dutton** | RAF No. 36071 | RAF | **BK877** | | A&AEE | † |
| **13.12.41** | F/L Arthur A.P. **Weller** | RAF No. 41507 | RAF | **HK823** | | 71 OTU | † |
| **17.12.41** | 1st Off L.O. **Mills** | - | (US)/ATA | **BJ440** | | 4 FPP | - |
| **18.01.42** | *no details available* | ? | ? | **BJ438** | | 301 MU | - |
| **26.01.42** | F/O Gerald **Dutton** | RAF No. 83506 | RAF | **BJ434** | | 15 FPP | - |
| **30.01.42** | Cap J.L. **Begg** | - | ATA | **AR671** | | 3 FPP | - |
| **01.02.42** | 1st Off F.D. **Carragher** | - | (US)/ATA | **AR664** | | 3 FPP | - |
| **04.02.42** | S/L Gordon R. **Fielder** | RAF No. 37764 | RAF | **BJ449** | | RAE | † |
| **07.04.42** | Sgt Kenneth A.G. **Prater** | RAF No. 1201795 | RAF | **AR685** | | Takoradi | - |
| **07.06.42** | *no details available* | ? | ? | **AX799** | | 301 MU | - |
| **22.02.43** | Sgt John T. **Strickland** | RAF No. 922262 | RAF | **AR635** | | 308 MU | - |
| **06.01.44** | F/Sgt Edward O. **Balls** | RAF No. 1147188 | RAF | **BJ532** | | 22 FC | - |
| **11.02.44** | P/O David W. **Davies** | RAF No. 168659 | RAF | **BJ539** | | 319 MU | - |
| **09.03.44** | *ground accident* | - | - | **AR633** | | 510 Sqn | - |

# With the SAAF

The SAAF would become a major user of the Mohawk but it would see little action. As stated in the introduction, the SAAF was in desperate need of modern fighters at the end of 1940. The SAAF was the backbone of the air component in East Africa fighting the Italians and the fighter force consisted of Hawker Furies, Gloster Gladiators and several Hawker Hurricanes. With the losses sustained during the Battle of Britain, the RAF could not provide many Hurricanes so the Mohawk was seen as an alternative as its performance was good enough to fight against the Italian Fiat CR.32 or CR42s. The first Mohawks were released early in 1941 and they were allocated serials from 2501 onwards, the first reaching Kenya in March 1941. In the followings weeks, 59 were taken on charge and, with the handing over of another fifteen in January and March 1943, 74 were received, but only seventy serials allocated (ending with 2570), meaning that not all were introduced into service. At least one would return to the RAF (AR669) after being with the SAAF between August and April 1941. The introduction into the SAAF was delayed, however, as powerplant defects were noted, specifically the oil system, and the aircraft were shipped back to England for remedial work. The Mohawks slowly began to return to Kenya in late April so conversion could finally begin. Number 4 Squadron was the first unit to convert. This unit was reformed at Waterkloof in South Africa on 24 March 1941 in response to a call for additional SAAF squadrons to be made available in the Middle East. This squadron soon moved to Nakuru in Kenya to work up. There they received their first Mohawks on 4 May and by June fourteen had been received (those known to have been used during that period are 2501, 2503, 2504, 2508 and 2510). The squadron then moved to Nanyuki on 10 July. Until the end of August, the unit trained on Mohawks even though engine defects limited flying and aerobatics were consequently forbidden. Later, the squadron relinquished its equipment in preparation for embarkation to Suez early in September.

At the same time No. 3 Squadron, which had fought in East Africa during the previous months, was in poor shape following its campaign with Gladiators and Hurricanes. Its B Flight was withdrawn to Nakuru and began to convert. Familiarisation started on 1 September and lasted one week but was not without incident. Captain Parsonson crashed on 2 September in 2510 owing to engine failure. He escaped injury. The first mission given to this flight was to maintain a presence near the protectorate of French

Three characters of the SAAF who flew Mohawks. Left, Captain 'Jack' Parsonson, who would be the only Commonwealth pilot to destroy an Axis aircraft while flying a Mohawk (even if it was on the ground). A regular SAAF officer, he would later serve in North Africa and became a PoW in May 1943 for the duration of the war. He was also awarded the DSO.

Bottom left, 'Jack' Frost was also a SA Permanent Force officer. He was, however, killed in action on 16 June 1942 while OC 5 Sqn SAAF. With sixteen confirmed kills, two being shared, Frost was the most successful SAAF pilot of W.W.II. He was also awarded the DFC and Bar.

Below right, 'Doug' Loftus, another member of the SA Permanent Forces, would become one of the 7 Wing SAAF wing leaders and eventually its OC as a colonel. He survived the war with a DSO and DFC. He continued to serve the SAAF after the war.

Two Mohawks ready for operations with 3 Sqn in East Africa, one of them suitably marked with the squadron badge. No individual letter markings seem to have been used during that period. Note the Gladiator behind the Mohawks.

Somaliland (Djibouti) from where it was known that an Italian Savoia S-75 was supplying Gondar. The flight (known as 41 Squadron Fighter Detachment for administrative purposes) moved to Ascia near the convergence of the French Somaliland, British Somaliland and Abyssinian borders. It lost two Mohawks, 2521 on the 9th and 2512 on the 14th, during the ferry flight with the latter overrunning the airfield when its flaps jammed. The pilot, 2/Lt Strong, was not hurt (he would be victim of another accident on take-off on the 28th in 2504). The next day, the 15th, the flight immediately began patrols to intercept the Savoia. Soon after, permission was granted to attack over the technically-neutral French territory if required. That permission would be used later on. On 4 October, the flight received information that the S-75 had landed at Djibouti. Captain Jack Parsonson immediately left to investigate but, in spite of this quick reaction, he saw nothing. He took off the next morning at 0745 in Mohawk 2522 and flew another unsuccessful sortie. He took off again at 1000 and luck was on his side this time when he saw the S-75 (with civil registration I-LUNO and bearing a Red Cross) parked in the open outside a hangar. He made two strafing runs over the Savoia and returned to base, leaving the Italian aircraft burning. This S-75 would actually be the only confirmed destruction of an Italian aircraft by a Mohawk during the East African campaign and was also the very first aircraft credited to a Mohawk in Commonwealth service. No one commented that an aircraft bearing a Red Cross should not be attacked, and it seems this was not reported by Parsonson. However, the S-75 was indeed flying partially illegal flights as it was ferrying out wounded personnel but flying in supplies on the return flights to Gondar. In the wreckage, condensed milk was found as well as mail. However, strafing the S-75 on the ground was a far better result than if it had been intercepted while ferrying wounded out of Gondar. Patrols continued along the French Somaliland border with little to report. On 15 October, the flight reverted to its previous identity as B Flight, 3 Squadron, and moved near Gondar to join the rest of the unit. From 9 November, operations commenced against Italians positions around Gondar with the Mohawks having been equipped with bomb racks in the meantime. The support was short, however, as Gondar finally fell on 27 November and brought the Italian resistance in East Africa to an end. The squadron began its move back to the Union soon after

Mohawks IVs of 4 Sqn SAAF at Nakuru in May 1941 during its conversion onto the type. The closest aircraft are 2503 and 2508.

with A Flight leaving first. B Flight remained until the end of December, being relocated to Ascia to resume patrols along the French Somaliland border. On 11 December, a French twin-engine fighter, a Potez 631, one of three (of four) still serving at Djibouti, flew over the South African camp at low level and Lt Gazzard, who had just taken off, gave chase. The French gunner opened fire, as did Gazzard who saw smoke coming from its left engine before the Potez dived into cloud and vanished. Gazzard would be credited with a damaged aircraft. The Potez returned to base safely where it was repaired. On 26 December, the flight almost lost a Mohawk when a patrol came under Vichy ground fire. The aircraft was hit in the fuselage and tailplane. A few days later, in January, the flight returned to the Union where it was disbanded and its surviving Mohawks were allocated to fighter training for units earmarked for home defence or Middle East service. The Mohawk made no substantial contribution to the outcome of the war in East Africa as it arrived too late to change anything. The type also became unpopular with the pilots because of the recurrent engine problems that had caused some losses during their passage to East Africa. The first loss occurred during a test flight on 27 September after an engine failure. Captain Jack Parsonson escaped injury. The next day, 2/Lt Strong crashed on take-off from Mega during a ferry flight after the controls jammed at 100 feet. He broke an arm and a leg and was repatriated to the Union for recovery. Two accidents, however, would have fatal consequences. Lieutenant A.C. Mitchell was killed during a non-operational flight when he crashed on take-off on 12 November and Mohawk 2545 burnt out. One week later it was the turn of Lt G.R. Jacobs to encounter the same fate in 2508 when he stalled on take-off for a patrol and crashed to his death. The known Mohawks used by 3 Squadron in East Africa are 2503, 2504, 2506, 2508, 2510, 2512, 2514, 2521, 2522, 2524, 2529, 2537 and 2545.

In the Union, the fighter force was also expanding. On 7 May 1941, No. 5 Squadron was reformed as a fighter squadron at Zwartkop near Pretoria and, initially, a great variety of generally obsolete aircraft were used. New equipment arrived in October with five Mohawks taken on charge (those known are 2501, 2503, 2516 and 2531). With them, the squadron, under the command of Major John Frost, began its operational training which continued until mid-December when the squadron received orders to move to North Africa. Number 7 Squadron was re-established on 12 January 1942 under the command of Major Doug Loftus. Again the unit was to work up with Mohawks prior to moving to the Middle East in April. During that time, various accidents were reported. On 19 February, 2/Lt A.B. Alexander crashed in 2511 while practicing an attack on a floating target. The pilot survived the crash but, two weeks later, another crash occurred (2518) and the pilot, Lt Engelbrecht, was killed. A final major accident took place on 5 May, when 2532 was wrecked during a crash. Its pilot, Capt Frank E. Adams, escaped major injury. The Mohawks known to have been issued are 2501, 2511, 2517, 2518, 2524, 2526, 2527, 2529, 2531, 2532, 2552, 2554, 2556 and 2559. In December 1941, with the outbreak of war against Japan, South Africa felt vulnerable to an attack from carrier aircraft along its Indian Ocean coastlines. This fear was soon confirmed when Ceylon was attacked on 5 March by aircraft operating from an aircraft carrier. In anticipation, No. 6 Squadron had been reformed on 1 February 1942 at Zwartkop under the command of Major Laurie Wilmot. He was soon replaced by Major Pieter Hayden-Thomas. Wilmot stayed on in charge of flight training. The squadron, from the beginning of April, progressively inherited the Mohawks left by No. 7 Squadron after its departure to the Middle East. In May, the squadron could count on nineteen Mohawks (other serials known are 2521, 2534 and 2540). On the 6th, the squadron moved to Grouville in Natal and, five days later, four Mohawks were sent to Stamford Hill in Durban where they immediately assumed standby. Patrols interspersed with training flights would become the daily routine for the next few weeks. The squadron reported its first loss, 2552 on 27 April, the pilot, Lt Clayton being safe followed by a second accident (2539) on 19 May with the pilot, 2/Lt J.G. Vermeulen, being

Mohawks IVs of 6 Sqn SAAF based at Durban with suburban houses in the background. In the foreground is Mohawk 2556, coded 'M'. Note this aircraft and the Mohawk behind, coded 'E', have two different art works painted ahead of the cockpit.

Number 6 Squadron Mohawk 2540/G being serviced. Note the squadron insignia painted ahead of the cockpit, a winged African spear pointed towards the ground - see colour profile -. *(Stefaan Bouwer)*

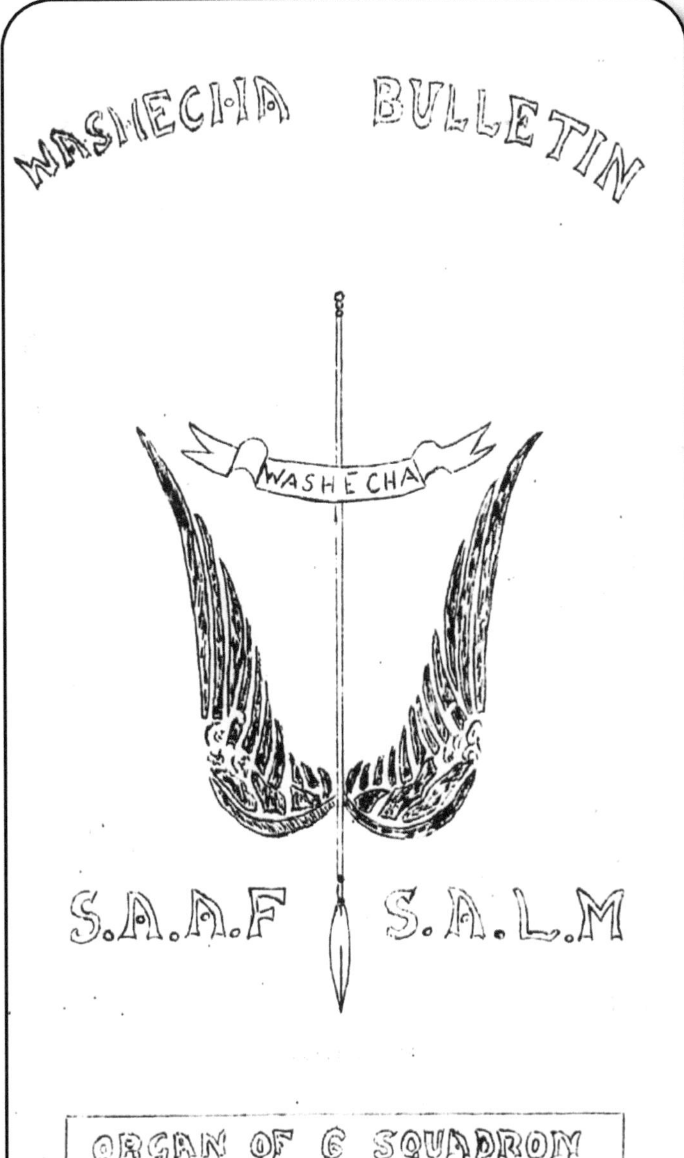


seriously injured. Two more Mohawks would be lost in the following days both after engine failure, but both pilots survived. At the end of May, fourteen Mohawks were transferred to the newly-formed No. 10 Squadron (among them were 2516, 2524, 2536, 2554 and 2556), leaving 6 Squadron with only five aircraft. Number 10 Squadron had been formed on 20 April under Capt Corry van Vliet as part of the coastal fighter force. This unit was now in charge of the defence of Cape Town. In spite of this deployment, on 20 May, a Japanese E14Y1 'Glen' floatplane, launched from the Japanese submarine I-10, overflew the port of Durban without being intercepted. This hostile flight was not the last as the Japanese floatplane reappeared during the following days without any reaction from the SAAF. This failure was caused by the delays between detection and the scramble order being received, hence the late arrival of a fighter response over the area. The squadron would only keep its Mohawks for a short time as it converted to Kittyhawks in June. The Mohawks were re-issued to 6 Squadron during July. The process hadn't been completed when 2556 crashed on take-off, hitting a fence and then a bungalow. Lieutenant V.V. Boyd was taken to hospital with facial injuries but would recover to serve with No. 92 Squadron RAF in Italy. The squadron would continue to perform coastal patrols with Mohawks until, with the diminished Japanese threat, it was disbanded on 28 July 1943, its A and C Flight becoming part of the newly established No. 11 OTU. One last Mohawk (2534) was lost during that time, on 13 August, and its pilot, 2/Lt I.L. Posenor, killed. In February of that year, the Mohawk Flight used 2538, 2560, 2561, 2562, 2563, 2564, 2565 and 2566. The other flight operated the Hawker Fury. It is worth noting that most Mohawks came from the last batch handed over by the RAF. The Mohawks were not used after the disbandment of 6 Squadron and were sent back to the Transvaal for storage as the SAAF finally had sufficient numbers of modern fighters to fill its needs. On 1 July 1944 there were 55 Mohawks on strength. Eleven were SOC the following 11 September and 43 on 22 November. The last one which was used as instructional aircraft at Air Schools (2569) would be struck off charge on 17 April 1946.

Left, the first 6 Squadron insignia adopted during the Mohawk era. See above Mohawk 2540/G

As always, incidents and accidents were part of the game with 2501/L and 2529/E having encountered some misfortune. Both returned to service.
*(Stefaan Bouwer)*

## Summary of the known aircraft lost by accident - SAAF

| Date | Pilot | S/N | Origin | Serial | Code | Unit | Fate |
|---|---|---|---|---|---|---|---|
| **02.09.41** | Capt John E. **Parsonson** | SAAF No. P102656 | SAAF | **2510** | | No. 3 Sqn* | - |
| **09.09.41** | 2/Lt Dennis C.C. **Gazzard** | SAAF No. 103289 | SAAF | **2521** | | No. 3 Sqn* | - |
| **14.09.41** | 2/Lt Peter F. **Strong** | SAAF No. 103280 | SAAF | **2512** | | No. 3 Sqn* | - |
| **27.09.41** | Capt John E. **Parsonson** | SAAF No. P102656 | SAAF | **2514** | | No. 3 Sqn* | - |
| **28.09.41** | 2/Lt Peter F. **Strong** | SAAF No. 103280 | SAAF | **2504** | | No. 3 Sqn* | - |
| **12.11.41** | Lt Alexander C. **Mitchell** | SAAF No. 103321 | SAAF | **2545** | | No. 3 Sqn | † |
| **20.11.41** | Lt Gabriel R. **Jacobs** | SAAF No. 103315 | SAAF | **2508** | | No. 3 Sqn | † |
| **06.03.42** | Lt August G.E.S. **Engelbrecht** | SAAF No. 103008 | SAAF | **2518** | | No. 7 Sqn | † |
| **27.04.42** | Lt John **Clayton** | SAAF No. 102339 | SAAF | **2552** | | No. 6 Sqn | - |
| **05.05.42** | Capt Frank E. **Adams** | SAAF No. 169730 | SAAF | **2532** | | No. 7 Sqn | - |
| **19.05.42** | 2/Lt Johannes G. **Vermeulen** | SAAF No. 143572 | SAAF | **2539** | | No. 6 Sqn | - |
| **20.05.42** | 2/Lt Aiden C. **Riley** | SAAF No. 236569 | SAAF | **2503** | | No. 6 Sqn | - |
| **25.05.42** | 2/Lt William R. **Sobey** | SAAF No. 205894 | SAAF | **2501** | | No. 6 Sqn | - |
| **27.07.42** | 2/Lt Vincent V. **Boy** | SAAF No. 205827 | SAAF | **2556** | | No. 6 Sqn | - |
| **13.08.42** | Lt Isaac L. **Posenor** | SAAF No. 206246 | SAAF | **2534** | | No. 6 Sqn | † |

**known as 41 Squadron Fighter Detachment*

**Another 6 Sqn Mohawk, coded 'T' (serial unknown), with Durban in the background.** *(Stefaan Bouwer)*

Mohawk 2535 had a very unusual career with the SAAF. What is known is that 2535 appears in a French pilot's logbook around October 1941. It is believed that it was borrowed in Egypt where the SAAF had sent some Mohawks to 71 OTU. It was not an official loan and we know that the Free French cross was painted on it (see photos). The Curtiss was taken back by the RAF in February 1942 needing an engine change (hence the photos top and middle) but no details have come to light about what happened next. However, we also know, from log-books, that the same aircraft was flown by the French during the next summer until August 1942. Was 2535 returned to the French in more acceptable markings with the roundels and rudder painted in French colours so as to get close to RAF regulations as per the last photo? It's a possibility.

# IN MEMORIAM

**Mohawk**

| *Name* | *Service No* | *Rank* | *Age* | *Origin* | *Date* | *Serial* |
|---|---|---|---|---|---|---|
| **Allen**, Derek Arthur | RAF No. 114662 | F/O | 23 | RAF | 28.01.43 | BT472 |
| **Blake**, Errol Walter Joseph | RAF No. 785051 | F/Sgt | *n/k* | (IRE)/RAF | 19.06.42 | BJ534 |
| **Boult**, Adam Desmond Stanley | RAF No. 1078250 | F/Sgt | 22 | RAF | 14.01.43 | BT471 |
| **Bugge**, Ronald | RAF No. 1294983 | F/Sgt | 20 | RAF | 28.10.43 | AR649 |
| **Cameron**, Robert Dyce | RAF No. 776154 | F/Sgt | 25 | RAF | 18.05.42 | BJ542 |
| **Campbell**, Christopher Gordon | RAF No. 1001167 | F/Sgt | 20 | RAF | 24.05.42 | BJ546 |
| **Chancellor**, Robert Nevin | NZ411859 | F/O | 29 | (UK)/RNZAF | 18.04.43 | BS790 |
| **Dutton**, John Edgar | RAF No. 36071 | S/L | 30 | RAF | 01.03.41 | BK877 |
| **Engelbrecht**, August Gottlieb Emiel Steffan | SAAF No. 103008 | Lt | *n/k* | SAAF | 06.03.42 | 2518 |
| **Fielder**, Gordon Rhodes | RAF No. 37764 | S/L | *n/k* | RAF | 04.02.42 | BJ449 |
| **Freeman**, Hubert Thomas | Aus. 404240 | P/O | 23 | RAAF | 20.04.43 | BK879 |
| **Gladwell**, John Mervyn | RAF No. 740551 | Sgt | 30 | RAF | 08.01.41 | AR651 |
| **Haley**, Allan Henry | Aus. 402054 | F/O | 25 | RAAF | 01.01.43 | BK584 |
| **Jacobs**, Gabriel Raymond | SAAF No. 103315 | Lt | *n/k* | SAAF | 20.11.41 | 2508 |
| **McClumpha**, Roy Colvin James | RAF No. 109781 | F/O | 25 | RAF | 10.11.42 | BB929 |
| **Mitchell**, Alexander Clifford | SAAF No. 103321 | Lt | *n/k* | SAAF | 12.11.43 | 2545 |
| **Posenor**, Isaac Leo | SAAF No. 206246 | Lt | *n/k* | SAAF | 13.08.42 | 2534 |
| **Potter**, George Bellenger | RAF No. 785062 | F/Sgt | 27 | (NZ)/RAF | 14.01.43 | AX893 |
| **Ross-Magenty**, Bruce Michael | RAF No. 118684 | F/L | 21 | RAF | 13.11.43 | AR677 |
| **Simpson**, James Alexander | RAF No. 946014 | F/Sgt | *n/k* | RAF | 20.04.43 | BK879 |
| **Squibb**, John Clive Dawson | RAF No. 85951 | F/O | *n/k* | RAF | 10.11.42 | AX898 |
| **Thomas**, William Geoffrey | RAF No. 655553 | F/Sgt | 22 | RAF | 30.09.42 | AX695 |
| **Tovey**, Richard Strangeways | RAF No. 111323 | F/O | *n/k* | RAF | 19.02.43 | BB977 |
| **Weller**, Arthur Adrian Percy | RAF No. 41507 | F/L | *n/k* | RAF | 13.12.41 | HK823 |
| **Wood**, Alan Tyson | RAF No. 785063 | Sgt | 27 | RAF | 24.05.42 | AR676 |

***Total: 25***

***Australia: 2, Ireland: 1, New Zealand: 1, South Africa: 4, United Kingdom: 17***

*n/k: not known*

Mohawk BT-471/H of No. 155 Sqn seen in 1942. Flight Sergeant Boult was killed in this aircraft on 14 January 1943.

**Curtiss Mohawk Mk. IV BJ546**

No. 5 Squadron

Dinjan (India), spring 1942

**Curtiss Mohawk Mk. IV AR690**
**No. 5 Squadron**
***Flight Sergeant Dick WICKS***
**Agartala (India), autumn 1942**

**Curtiss Mohawk Mk. IV BS796**

**No. 5 Squadron**

***Squadron Leader Peter M. BOND***

**Agartala (India), beginning 1943**

**Curtiss Mohawk Mk. IV BB928**

**No. 155 Squadron**

***Squadron Leader Charles G. St.D 'Porky' JEFFRIES***

**Agartala (India), beginning 1943**

**(aircraft shown while being under repainting process)**

**Curtiss Mohawk Mk. IV AR674**

**No. 155 Squadron**

***Flying Officer Lloyd T. HUNTER***

**Agartala (India), summer 1943**

**Curtiss Mohawk Mk. IV BS790**
**No. 169 Wing**
***Squadron Leader William PITT-BROWN***
**Agartala (India), November 1942**

**Curtiss Mohawk Mk. IV 2540**
**No. 6 Squadron SAAF**
**Durban (South Africa), Summer 1942**

# SQUADRONS! - The series

1 The Supermarine Spitfire Mk VI
2 The Republic Thunderbolt Mk I
3 The Supermarine Spitfire Mk V in the Far East
4 The Boeing Fortress Mk I
5 The Supermarine Spitfire Mk XII
6 The Supermarine Spitfire Mk VII
7 The Supermarine Spitfire F. 21
8 The Handley-Page Halifax Mk I
9 The Forgotten Fighters
10 The NA Mustang IV in Western Europe
11 The NA Mustang IV over the Balkans and Italy
12 The Supermarine Spitfire Mk XVI - *The British*
13 The Martin Marauder Mk I
14 The Supermarine Spitfire Mk VIII in the Southwest Pacific - *The British*
15 The Gloster Meteor F.I & F.III
16 The NA Mitchell - *The Dutch, Poles and French*
17 The Curtiss Mohawk
18 The Curtiss Kittyhawk Mk II
19 The Boulton Paul Defiant - *day and night fighter*
20 The Supermarine Spitfire Mk VIII in the Southwest Pacific - The Australians
21 The Boeing Fortress Mk II & Mk III
22 The Douglas Boston and Havoc - *The Australians*
23 The Republic Thunderbolt Mk II
24 The Douglas Boston and Havoc - *Night fighters*
25 The Supermarine Spitfire Mk V - *The Eagles*
26 The Hawker Hurricane - The Canadians
27 The Supermarine Spitfire Mk V - *The 'Bombay' squadrons*
28 The Consolidated Liberator - *The Australians*
29 The Supermarine Spitfire Mk XVI - *The Dominions*
30 The Supermarine Spitfire Mk V - *The Belgian and Dutch squadrons*
31 The Supermarine Spitfire Mk V - *The New-Zealanders*
32 The Supermarine Spitfire Mk V - *The Norwegians*
33 The Brewster Buffalo
34 The Supermarine Spitfire Mk II - *The Foreign squadrons*
35 The Martin Marauder Mk II
36 The Supermarine Spitfire Mk V - *The Special Reserve squadrons*
37 The Supermarine Spitfire Mk XIV - *The Belgian and Dutch squadrons*
38 The Supermarine Spitfire Mk II - *The Rhodesian, Dominion & Eagle squadrons*
39 The Douglas Boston and Havoc - *Intruders*
40 The North American Mustang Mk III over Italy and the Balkans (Pt-1)
41 The Bristol Brigand
42 The Supermarine Spitfire Mk V - *The Australians*
43 The Hawker Typhoon - *The Rhodesian squadrons*
44 The Supermarine Spitfire F.22 & F.24
45 The Supermarine Spitfire Mk IX - *The Belgian and Dutch squadrons*
46 The North American & CAC Mustang - *The RAAF*
47 The Westland Whirlwind
48 The Supermarine Spitfire Mk XIV - *The British squadrons*
49 The Supermarine Spitfire Mk I - *The beginning (the Auxiliary squadrons)*
50 The Hawker Tempest Mk V - *The New Zealanders*
51 The Last of the Long-Range Biplane Flying Boats
52 The Supermarine Spitfire Mk IX - *The Former Canadian Homefront squadrons*
53 The Hawker Hurricane Mk I & Mk II - *The Eagle squadrons*
54 The Hawker biplane fighters
55 The Supermarine Spitfire Mk IX - *The Auxiliary squadrons*
56 The Hawker Typhoon - *The Canadian squadrons*
57 The Douglas SBD - *New Zealand and France*
58 The Forgotten Patrol Seaplanes
59 The Dutch Fighter Squadrons - *Nos. 322 & 120 (NEI) Squadrons*
60 The Supermarine Spitfire - *The Australian Squadrons in Western Europe and the Med*

Printed in the USA
CPSIA information can be obtained
at www.ICGtesting.com
CBHW041711061224
18620CB00024B/409
* 9 7 9 1 0 9 6 4 9 0 0 0 4 *